Supporting Multilingual Learners

50 STRATEGIES for Language and Literacy Instruction

HEINEMANN
Portsmouth, NH

Acknowledgments:
Lexile® is a trademark of MetaMetrics, Inc., and is registered in the United States and abroad. Mad Libs® is a registered trademark of Penguin Random House LLC. Jeopardy!® is a trademark of Jeopardy Productions, Inc. Trivial Pursuit® is a registered trademark of Hasbro, Inc. Google Translate™ is a trademark of Google LLC.

Acknowledgments continue on page 190.

Library of Congress Cataloging-in-Publication Data
Names: Moses, Lindsey, author.
Title: Supporting multilingual learners : 50 strategies for language and literacy instruction / Lindsey Moses.
Description: Portsmouth, NH : Heinemann, 2024. | Includes bibliographical references.
Identifiers: LCCN 2024010639 | ISBN 9780325161174
Subjects: LCSH: Linguistic minorities—Education—United States. | Limited English proficient students—United States. | Literacy—Study and teaching—United States. | English language—Study and teaching—United States. | Language arts—Correlation with content subjects—United States.
Classification: LCC LC3731 .S88 2024 | DDC 370.117/50973—dc23/eng/20240508
LC record available at https://lccn.loc.gov/2024010639

Printed in the U.S.A. on acid-free paper

ISBN-13: 978-0-325-16117-4

1 2 3 4 5 6 7 8 9 10 VP 29 28 27 26 25 24

4500893486 r9.24

Acquisitions Editor: Zoë Ryder White
Production Editor: Victoria Merecki
Cover Designer: Suzanne Heiser
Interior Designer and Typesetter: Shawn Girsberger
Front Cover Image: © Malte Mueller/Getty Images
Author Photo: Frank Serafini
Manufacturing: Jaime Spaulding
Permissions: David Stockdale

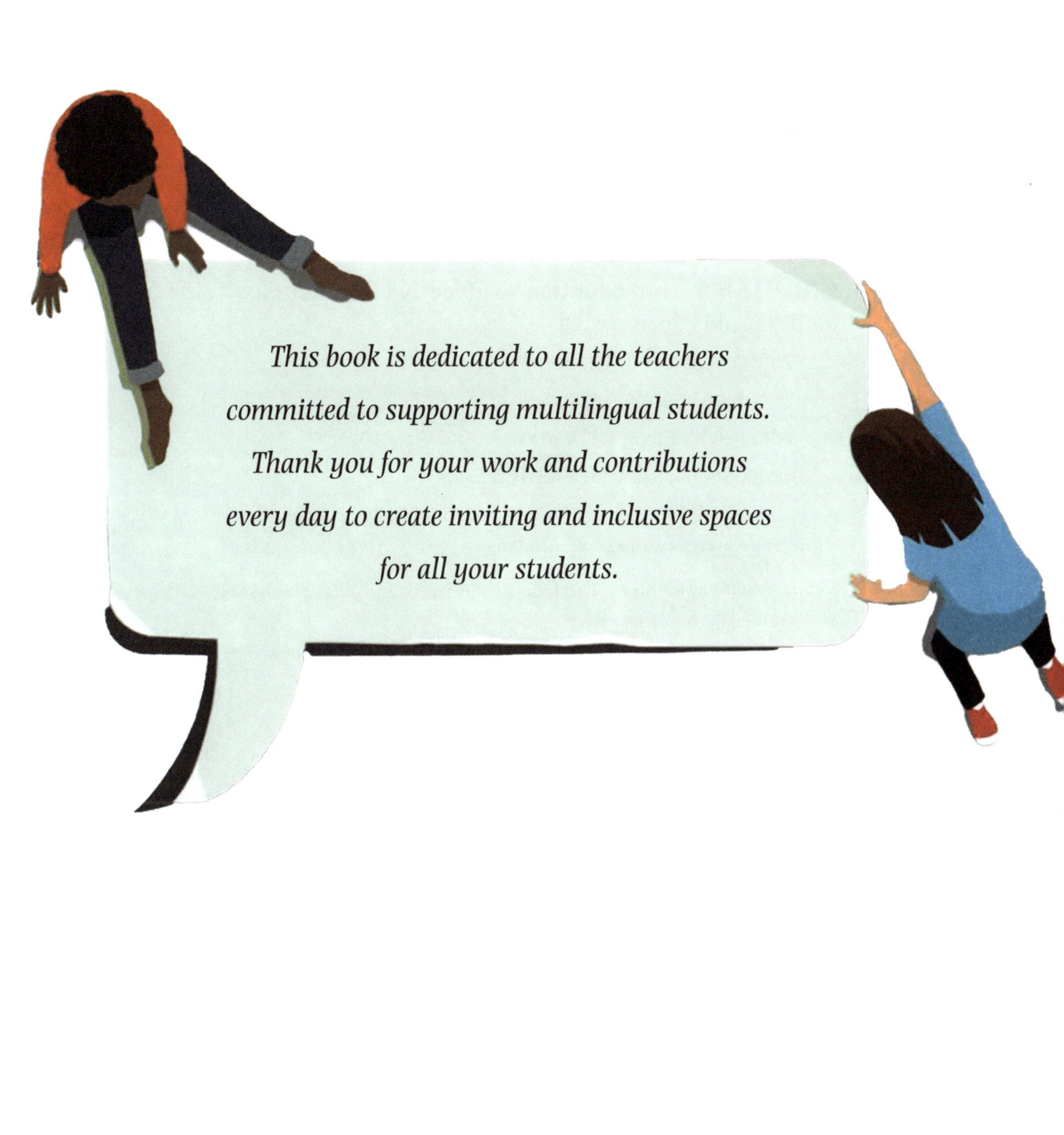
This book is dedicated to all the teachers committed to supporting multilingual students. Thank you for your work and contributions every day to create inviting and inclusive spaces for all your students.

CONTENTS

ONLINE RESOURCES CONTENTS

How to Access the Online Resources

1. Go to **http://hein.pub/Multilingual-login**.
2. Log in with your username and password. If you do not already have an account with Heinemann, you will need to create an account.
3. On the Welcome page, choose "**Click here to register an Online Resource.**"
4. Register your product by entering the code **SCAFFOLDS** (be sure to read and check the acknowledgment box under the keycode).
5. Once you have registered your product, it will appear alphabetically in your account list under "**My Online Resources.**"

Note: When returning to Heinemann.com to access your previously registered products, simply log in to your Heinemann account and click on "**View my registered Online Resources.**"

ACKNOWLEDGMENTS

This book would not have been possible without the collaboration of many educators and their students. Cat Frayne, Paula Garces, Matt Hajdun, Dana Cheriff, Tam Jarowyj, and Rachel Frevert, thank you for inviting me into your classrooms and sharing your brilliant ideas and student work with me—they made this book exponentially better. A huge thank-you to the Columbus School in Medellín, Colombia, for your continued collaboration and willingness to think together and share the thoughtful work that happens in your school. Sindy Villamizar, your thoughtful Spanish instruction inspired me to think deeper about ways we could provide your level of instruction for large groups of multilingual students. Thanks also to Tanny McGregor for sharing her beautiful sketchnote.

I am so thankful for the time, collaboration, research, and writing opportunities supported by the University of South Australia. It was a wonderful intellectual space that inspired me during the writing of this book.

Finally, this book was ultimately possible because of the support of three people: Holly Kim Price, Zoë White, and Frank Serafini. Holly, thank you for being a thought partner during the early stages of the book when I needed you to help me conceptualize and narrow the focus. Zoë, thanks for taking on this project and providing encouragement, patience, and feedback that all made this a better book. Frank, I can't even begin to list all the ways you supported me through this book. It was a wild year, and your intellectual support was surpassed only by your encouragement and willingness to take on all the things at home to make sure I had time and space to commit to writing this book. Thank you!

Introduction to Effective Literacy Scaffolds for Multilingual Learners

Why Do We Need This Book?

Over 50 percent of the world's population is now bilingual and using their bilingualism as an asset in the evolving global economy (Grosjean 2010). Students who are fortunate enough to speak English as an additional language are a quickly growing demographic in public schools in the United States. New and veteran teachers report being eager to learn new and effective strategies to support their students who speak languages other than English at home. Many multilingual learners find a great deal of academic success, but the data does suggest that as an educational community, we have room to improve when thinking about designing and implementing effective instruction specifically targeted for supporting multilingual learners (Correia 2020).

Unfortunately, multilingual learners have historically received instruction that has focused on decontextualized, rote-based acquisition of skills and content (Allington 1991; Darling-Hammond 1995).

Multilingual learners have also been frequently placed in lower-ability groups with an emphasis on language as a form, where they are unable to draw on background knowledge, topics of interest, and motivation (Ruiz-de-Velasco and Fix 2000; Bernhardt 2011). More recent research shows that multilingual learners benefit from instruction that involves meaningful, content-rich activities that encourage language growth through engagement, discussion, and cocreation of academic products (Hakuta and Santos 2012, iii). While many scholars have documented the institutional marginalization of multilingual learners, other recent research documents classroom practices that create opportunities for positive identity development and academic progress for multilingual learners (Moses and Kelly 2017, 2018).

In this book, I aim to share practical instructional scaffolds and strategies that focus on inclusive and supportive practices for multilingual learners, garnered from my research and collaboration with exemplary teachers. Multiple instructional strategies might be used in a single lesson to scaffold complex thinking and tasks, so this book is designed to share five instructional strategies for each research-based scaffold so that teachers have plenty of options when making instructional decisions based on their unique students' needs.

Language Learning

The reality is that learning another language is hard. As someone who has committed my work and research to learning about language acquisition and effective instructional strategies, I am constantly reflecting on my own second language learning. A couple of years ago, I began one-on-one video conference tutoring two to three times a week with Sindy Villamizar, a Spanish teacher in Colombia. While I am highly critical of my own progress, I am always inspired by her thoughtful instruction, which manages to help me celebrate successes and nudge me to think about the next linguistic nuance. Her instruction is purposeful, individualized, and always targeted to just what I seem to need in that context. This experience is humbling and yet exactly what I need as I explore more effective approaches to supporting children who are learning an additional language. Unfortunately, not all instruction can take place in one-on-one settings, so I continue to ask myself, *How can we take individualized language scaffolds and supports and make them accessible to teachers working with a classroom full of students?*

As I work and learn alongside many schools and individual educators who are committed to supporting children as they learn English, I am constantly reminded that this work is challenging and messy, and it differs for every child. I have spent the last ten years researching, teaching, and consulting on this topic, and I believe we need to take a closer look at the scaffolds we use to support students who are learning an additional language. However, we can't talk abstractly about scaffolding for students. We need practical, classroom-tested, research-supported instructional scaffolds specifically designed to support students who speak multiple languages.

Who Are Multilingual Learners?

According to the most recent data from the National Center for Education Statistics (2023), nearly five million students were classified as English language learners (I refer to these students as *multilingual learners*) in US public schools in the fall of 2020. These numbers reflect students who had not yet reached English language proficiency according to the state assessments and made up 10.3 percent of US public school students. While Spanish remains the most common home language of multilingual learners (75.5 percent), there are over four hundred languages spoken at home by multilingual learners in the US (Bialik, Scheller, and Walker 2018).

While multilingual learners all have the process of learning another language in common, they are a unique group of individuals. Like any group of learners, they have different backgrounds, beliefs, preferences, personalities, knowledge bases, needs, and strengths. Teachers can support these strengths by providing culturally and linguistically sustaining instruction and assessment (Paris 2012). This involves teachers recognizing, responding to, and validating students' cultural practices through multimodal and multilingual learning opportunities.

I want to take a brief moment to talk about terminology. Many terms and labels have been used to identify students in US schools who are learning English. I celebrate and support bilingualism, so I most frequently refer to students as *bilingual students* or *emerging bilinguals* in my research writing as a way to honor and celebrate the multiple languages children speak. However, this term is often criticized or confused in both research literature and practitioner literature because it is not always representative of the types and models of instruction that students receive. For example, if the instructional methodologies being suggested are specifically for helping students learn English (not promoting simultaneous bilingualism), then critics would argue that the terminology, like *multilingual learner*, should be aligned with the instructional model. While I fully support bilingual education whenever possible, the purpose of this book is to support teachers who are providing instruction in English to multilingual learners learning English. *English learner (EL)* and *English language learner (ELL)* are the two most prominent terms used in federal, state, and local educational contexts and policies, but these terms fail to recognize the fact that students are often learning multiple languages. These terms also position English as more important than other languages, thus devaluing the many linguistic resources multilingual learners bring from other languages. For clarity and the aforementioned reasons, I have decided to use the term *multilingual learner* throughout the book.

Foundational Principles for This Book

All of my work is grounded in sociocultural theory (Vygotsky 1978/1995; Wertsch 1998; Lave and Wenger 1991) and the belief that all learning (language, literacy, content) is situated in a social context. Children learn language with, from, and alongside other people. They are unique individuals, and teachers can support them best by making connections, building relationships, and getting to know them in a holistic way. There is no one perfect approach for all multilingual learners—or any students for that matter. My goal with this book is to provide practical strategies you can use flexibly within a classroom context that puts multilingual learners' learning front and center, so the content of this book is guided by three principles: assets-based approaches to teaching and learning; language-oriented planning, instruction, and assessment; and meaningful interactive opportunities for authentic language use.

Assets-Based Approaches to Teaching and Learning

Historically, schools often viewed multilingual learners from a position of what they did not have: English proficiency or proficient performance on English assessments. I have heard teachers say things like, "They don't have background knowledge." I always reply that multilingual students have more background knowledge and experiences than we could ever imagine. All of our students come with many cultural and linguistic resources, and it is our job to build on those "funds of knowledge" (Moll et al. 1992) and simultaneously support their ability to communicate those resources in English when their teacher and peers do not speak their home language. I view and frame all second language learning stages and processes as assets. Multilingual learners bring so many assets from their home language and experiences, *and* they are also learning English and academic content in English in school. That is impressive! All assets-based instruction begins with identification of what multilingual learners know, and the goals of all instruction are situated in what students can and will be able to do.

In addition to educational settings, bilingualism has many documented benefits. People who speak multiple languages experience cognitive benefits such as increased attention span and ability to multitask, lessened cognitive decline with age, and delays in dementia and Alzheimer's onset (Bialystok 2011). People who speak multiple languages have the opportunity to participate as global citizens who can communicate in multiple contexts with a wider range of people than their monolingual peers. Being bilingual also increases workplace marketability in an increasingly global society.

Language-Oriented Planning, Instruction, and Assessment

If we want to support multilingual learners, we must be equipped with the tools to design and implement language-oriented instruction and assessment. This means we need to have an understanding of students' language proficiency levels and the stages of language acquisition. We must plan for supported authentic experiences to build on current strengths to develop their language in reading, writing, speaking, and listening. This is so much more than thinking about adding extra vocabulary words. This means purposefully planning which scaffolds to utilize to help multilingual learners gain access to grade-level content and whole-group instruction, but it also means planning ways students, even at the beginning stages of English language proficiency, can participate and document what they know because they know a lot. I address considerations for scaffolds to support language-oriented whole-group, collaborative, independent, small-group, and conferring experiences throughout the book.

Meaningful Interactive Opportunities for Authentic Language Use

If we want students to learn a language, we have to plan time for them to use it. Whole-group instruction often involves the teacher speaking, modeling, and possibly asking for brief input from the students. This might include hand raising and one or two students giving responses, or it might include a brief think-pair-share. Then, teachers often send students off to work independently. For students learning English, particularly students who are more reluctant to speak, this means they rarely have opportunities to speak and further develop their oral language in English. It is essential to plan for and build in scaffolds that include wait time, supported oral language structures, and talk-equity considerations in every whole-group and small-group experience we design for multilingual learners.

What Are Scaffolds?

Most educators are familiar with the term *scaffolding*, though different scholars and resources define it in different ways. Outside educational contexts, people typically associate scaffolds with temporary structures used in the process of constructing a building. In relation to education, the term was originally used by Wood, Bruner, and Ross (1976) as a metaphor when studying parent-child talk in the early years, and they describe it as "the steps taken to reduce the degrees of freedom in carrying out some tasks so that the child can concentrate on the difficult skills she is in the process of acquiring" (19). However, many scholars are quick to note that it is not as simple as just helping a child complete a task (Maybin, Mercer, and Stierer 1992); rather, it is temporary and specific assistance from a teacher or mentor that will enable the student to complete similar tasks alone in the future (Gibbons 2002).

Scaffolding has long been discussed in relation to Vygotsky's zone of proximal development (ZPD) because he argued that learning takes place when the learner needs teacher, adult, or mentor support. It is in this zone that students learn and move toward independence, thanks to the assistance—or what Wood, Bruner, and Ross (1976) referred to as scaffolding—from knowledgeable others (typically adults). At the core of this work is the idea that instead of simplifying the task for the child, we should adjust the scaffold we're providing to support the learner in accomplishing this task, initially with the scaffolds and then eventually on their own without scaffolds. Originally, this work and research focused specifically on monolingual speakers but more recently has begun to focus on supporting multilingual learners as well (Cummins 2000; Gibbons 2002, 2009; Krashen 2003).

There are many ways to think about and categorize scaffolds. For example, Marsh (2018) categorizes scaffolds for meaning making into three categories: visual aids, modeling practices, and a wide range of presentation strategies. Diane Staehr Fenner (2019) also has three categories, but they are materials and resources, instruction, and student grouping. WIDA (2012) uses the terms *sensory supports*, *graphic supports*, and *interactive supports*. WIDA also differentiates between macroscaffolding practices and microscaffolding practices. Macroscaffolding practices are preplanned scaffolds based on a long-term vision and sequence used in the instruction, and microscaffolding practices are provided during lessons through interactions between the teacher and student based on student need in the moment.

For the purposes of this book, I use the term *scaffold* to represent a broad category or type of scaffold (see the list of ten in the next section), but within each scaffold I include instructional strategies that fit within that category. For example, *Use visuals to support understanding* is a scaffold, and within that scaffold I might introduce the following instructional strategies: (1) Use pictures and realia to introduce vocabulary and build background about a new topic; (2) Provide emergent speakers with an image bank to respond to questions and participate in discussion; (3) Incorporate video with closed captioning to support and reinforce concepts; (4) Introduce complex concepts with graphic organizers to assist in broader understanding and connections across concepts; and (5) Use color-coding on presentations and documents (for example, to highlight vocabulary, draw attention to grammatical patterns, reinforce newly learned prefixes and suffixes, introduce and reinforce tenses, highlight cognates, or identify similar and different characteristics).

These instructional strategies are easy to implement but can make a large difference in helping your students have greater access to complex concepts and tools to help communicate their understanding in linguistically appropriate ways. Throughout the book I provide suggestions and share classroom examples of how I and other teachers used these instructional strategies.

Ten Research-Based, Easy-to-Use Scaffolds

Students are unique and need a wide range of scaffolds to support their learning. These might range from multiple and highly supportive scaffolds for beginning multilingual learners to one very light scaffold for nearly proficient English speakers. It is important to remember that scaffolds are beneficial during instruction as a way to help students access the content, but they are equally as important in helping students document and share their learning. During any given lesson, I might use a variety of scaffolds depending on my instructional purpose and students' needs. Research has reported these scaffolds as being highly effective for multilingual students (August, Fenner, and Snyder 2014; Goldenberg 2013).

1. Connect new learning to prior learning and experiences.
2. Teach academic vocabulary.
3. Model skills, strategies, and procedures.
4. Use visuals to support understanding.
5. Adjust speech and time.
6. Provide repeated exposure and opportunities for practice.
7. Prepare resources to support student responses (sentence stems, word banks, etc.).
8. Prepare structured oral language opportunities with talk-equity considerations.
9. Connect to and build on students' home language skills and knowledge.
10. Draw attention to language and expanding grammatical complexity.

Stages of Language Proficiency

To get the biggest benefit from these scaffolds, we must know what our students can do and when and where they might need support to meet the challenges. There are many considerations, but language and literacy proficiency are two key areas that should inform our decisions about scaffolding and instructional strategies. Most schools require a great deal of data collection and assessments related to ongoing literacy development, but teachers often have far less training on thinking about second language proficiency and development. I find the WIDA website to be a wonderful free resource for educators working with multilingual students.

In Figure 1.1, you will see the general performance definitions for the levels of English language proficiency (WIDA Consortium 2007), but you can also find grade-level-specific "can-do descriptors," which are broken down into language domain (listening, speaking, reading, and writing), on the WIDA website. I find these to be particularly helpful as teachers are becoming more familiar with what students at their grade level and language proficiency level *can* do. This also helps teachers see what they will be working toward to move to the next level. Scaffolds play a crucial role in helping students access and move toward that next level.

Performance definitions for the levels of English language proficiency

At the given level of English language proficiency, English language learners will process, understand, produce, or use

6 Reaching	› specialized or technical language reflective of the content area at grade level; › a variety of sentence lengths of varying linguistic complexity in extended oral or written discourse as required by the specified grade level; › oral or written communication in English comparable to proficient English peers
5 Bridging	› the technical language of the content areas; › a variety of sentence lengths of varying linguistic complexity in extended oral or written discourse, including stories, essays, or reports; › oral or written language approaching comparability to that of English proficient peers when presented with grade level material
4 Expanding	› specific and some technical language of the content areas; › a variety of sentence lengths of varying linguistic complexity in oral discourse or multiple, related paragraphs; › oral or written language with minimal phonological, syntactic, or semantic errors that do not impede the overall meaning of the communication when presented with oral or written connected discourse with occasional visual and graphic support
3 Developing	› general and some specific language of the content areas; › expanded sentences in oral interaction or written paragraphs; › oral or written language with phonological, syntactic, or semantic errors that may impede the communication but retain much of its meaning when presented with oral or written, narrative or expository descriptions with occasional visual and graphic support
2 Beginning	› general language related to the content areas; › phrases or short sentences; › oral or written language with phonological, syntactic, or semantic errors that often impede the meaning of the communication when presented with one to multiple-step commands, directions, questions, or a series of statements with visual and graphic support
1 Entering	› pictorial or graphic representation of the language of the content areas; › words, phrases, or chunks of language when presented with one-step commands, directions, WH-questions, or statements with visual and graphic support

FIGURE 1.1 *WIDA Performance Definitions*

How This Book Is Organized

This book is organized by a series of ten primary scaffolds. Each chapter focuses on one of the ten research-based scaffolds and includes five easy-to-use instructional strategies that fit within that scaffold. The chapters begin with a glimpse into the classroom followed by a brief overview of the scaffold. Then you will find five strategies, each of which includes a brief and practical description along with suggestions for when and with whom you might use this strategy. The next section, "Strategies in Action," provides a classroom example of the strategy in use in either a primary or an intermediate grade. I share the reality of how the implementation of the instructional strategy went and also describe the on-the-spot, individualized instructional strategies we used during the lesson based on students' needs. The chapters end with reflection questions.

Instructional Goals Supported by the Strategies

The chapters are organized by research-based scaffolds with five instructional strategies. Figure 1.2 provides another way to navigate this book. You can identify instructional goals you want to address

	STRATEGY	Speaking	Listening	Reading	Writing	Supporting understanding and access to content and skills	Supporting ways students can document learning and knowledge	Building and retaining vocabulary	Building and connecting to background knowledge	Supporting oral language development	Expanding linguistic complexity
CHAPTER 2	S1	•	•	•	•	•	•		•		
	S2	•	•	•	•	•			•	•	
	S3	•	•			•			•		
	S4	•	•	•	•	•	•		•		
	S5	•	•	•	•		•	•	•		
CHAPTER 3	S1	•	•	•	•	•	•	•	•		•
	S2	•	•	•	•		•	•	•	•	
	S3	•	•	•				•		•	
	S4	•	•	•		•		•	•		•
	S5	•	•	•			•	•	•	•	
CHAPTER 4	S1		•	•		•		•			
	S2		•	•		•			•		
	S3	•	•	•	•	•	•	•			
	S4	•	•	•	•	•	•			•	
	S5	•	•	•	•	•	•			•	•
CHAPTER 5	S1		•			•		•	•		
	S2					•		•	•		
	S3			•	•	•	•	•			
	S4		•	•	•	•	•	•			
	S5	•	•	•	•	•	•	•	•	•	•
CHAPTER 6	S1		•			•					
	S2	•	•			•	•				
	S3	•	•	•	•		•				
	S4	•	•	•		•		•			
	S5	•	•	•	•	•	•	•	•	•	

FIGURE 1.2 *Instructional Goal Organization Chart*

and then see the list of applicable strategies throughout the book. Most strategies will address multiple or all of the goals, but the • delineates the focal goals.

	STRATEGY	Speaking	Listening	Reading	Writing	Supporting understanding and access to content and skills	Supporting ways students can document learning and knowledge	Building and retaining vocabulary	Building and connecting to background knowledge	Supporting oral language development	Expanding linguistic complexity
CHAPTER 7	S1	•	•	•		•		•			
	S2	•	•	•			•	•			
	S3	•	•	•	•	•	•	•		•	
	S4	•	•	•	•	•	•				
	S5	•	•	•	•	•	•	•			
CHAPTER 8	S1	•	•	•	•	•	•	•		•	
	S2	•	•	•	•		•			•	•
	S3	•	•	•	•	•	•				
	S4			•	•	•	•	•			•
	S5		•	•	•	•	•	•	•		
CHAPTER 9	S1	•	•				•			•	•
	S2	•	•				•			•	•
	S3	•	•				•			•	•
	S4	•	•				•			•	•
	S5	•	•	•	•	•	•	•	•	•	•
CHAPTER 10	S1	•	•	•				•	•		
	S2	•	•	•	•	•		•	•		
	S3	•	•	•	•	•			•		
	S4	•	•	•	•	•	•		•		•
	S5	•	•	•	•	•	•		•	•	
CHAPTER 11	S1	•	•	•	•	•	•				•
	S2	•	•	•	•	•	•		•	•	•
	S3	•	•	•	•	•	•			•	•
	S4	•	•	•	•	•	•				•
	S5	•	•	•	•	•	•				•

FIGURE 1.2 *Instructional Goal Organization Chart*

Connect New Learning to Prior Learning and Experiences

VIGNETTE

Maria, a new second-grade teacher, started an integrated science and literacy (informational text) unit on rainforests. She decided to introduce the unit by building on students' background knowledge and doing a whole-class KWL chart. She told the students they would be reading, writing, and learning about rainforests in science and literacy.

> **Maria:** *We are going to write down what we already know about rainforests, so take a minute to think, and then in small groups you will add your ideas to the chart.*

Students in group 1 elected Sarah to be the recorder (person to write on their graphic organizer).

> **Abir:** *Lots of rain.* [Sarah wrote it on the chart.]
>
> **Samantha:** *Snakes.* [Sarah wrote it on the chart.]
>
> **Paul:** *That is where toucans live.* [Sarah wrote it on the chart.]

Eduardo: *Toucans can't fly because their beak is too big.* [Sarah paused.]

Paul: *They can fly. They are birds.*

Eduardo: *So is an ostrich, but they can't fly. The beak is too heavy to fly; it is bigger than the body.*

Paul: *Oh, OK.* [Sarah wrote, "Toucans can't fly," on the chart.]

During plan time later that week, Maria shared the dilemma of students writing things in the K ("What I Know") column that were inaccurate. She asked what the other teachers did when that happened. One of her colleagues said they did not correct these misconceptions because they were the students' background knowledge, and they should encounter the correct answer throughout the unit. Another colleague said that they would ask if the students knew something for certain and suggest it might be an idea to go in the W ("What I Want to Know") column for further exploration. The third colleague said, "That is why I stopped using the KWL. It does get them to identify background knowledge, but it feels so black and white with what they knew before and then after without a lot of room for approximations or changing thinking. I have changed to the RAN chart instead. I can share it with you." (I explain the reading and analyzing nonfiction [RAN] chart in greater depth later.)

What Does the Research Say?

As you can see in the previous vignette, not all scaffolds work well with all students in all contexts. One important aspect of identifying students' background knowledge, experiences, and prior learning is acknowledging that their current understandings will and should evolve and change over time with new learning. Research has documented that building on students' background knowledge and experiences is an effective scaffold to introduce additional material and content that will deepen and extend their knowledge (Goldenberg 2013).

There are many ways to connect new learning to prior learning, but all of them require first knowing about students and their experiences, knowledge, and interests. Moll et al. (1992) recommend using a theory called funds of knowledge to build a bridge of understanding between the classroom and resources and knowledge students possess at home and in their lives outside of school. The idea is to approach learning about students and their communities from an assets-based perspective with the understanding that all people are competent and have skills in various contexts. Building on the many funds of knowledge students possess has been documented to have several positive effects, including improved relationships between students and teachers (Barton and Tan 2009) and improved academic learning (Subero, Vujasinović, and Esteban-Guitart 2017).

Five Instructional Strategies

The instructional strategies throughout this chapter draw on the research findings to provide multiple approaches to identifying and building on students' background knowledge and prior experiences to connect to new learning.

STRATEGY 1 RAN Chart with Multilingual Adaptations

The KWL chart (Ogle 1986) is a popular graphic organizer teachers use to encourage students to document what they know (K), what they want to know (W), and what they have learned after reading (L). While this strategy does connect new learning to prior learning and experiences, it can come with some challenges, as seen in the opening vignette. For example, what do you do if a student thinks they know something, but the information is inaccurate?

The reading and analyzing nonfiction (RAN) chart (Stead 2005) remedies some of these challenges by including five columns. Stead's version incorporates activating prior knowledge before reading, confirming and reevaluating that prior knowledge while reading, noting new information learned, and asking questions (see Figure 2.1).

What I Think I Know	Confirmed	Misconceptions	New Learning	Wonderings

FIGURE 2.1 *Reading and Analyzing Nonfiction Chart*

For multilingual students, this decreases the anxiety of being right and having to know something for certain and celebrates moving information from the "What I Think I Know" column to the "Misconceptions" column. You can use this instructional strategy with the whole class, small groups, or individuals.

I have seen adapted language for the columns, depending on grade level. For example:

1. What I Think I Know
2. Confirmed
3. I Don't Think This Anymore *or* Not Quite
4. Exciting New Information *or* I Learned
5. Questions; I Wonder; *or* I Am Still Curious About

For multilingual students, I adapted this chart to include a "Connections" column and sentence stems to help students get started when documenting their thinking. Another modification for multilingual students is asking them to sketch an image with their writing in the graphic organizer (see Figure 2.2 and OR 2–1 in the Online Resources).

OR 2-1	
READING AND ANALYZING NONFICTION CHART FOR MULTILINGUALS	
Name:	
What I Think I Know	I think I know
Confirmed Knowledge	
Misconceptions	
Connections to My Life, Other Text, or the World	This reminds me of
Questions	Who, what, when, where, and why . . . ? I wonder
New Learning	I learned

FIGURE 2.2 *Reading and Analyzing Nonfiction Chart for Multilinguals* **OR 2-1**

Steps for instruction

1. Create an adapted RAN chart with language appropriate for your students' age and language proficiency level in large format (poster, whiteboard, or online interactive tool such as a digital whiteboard).
2. Explain that building background knowledge helps readers connect to the text and integrate new information and learning

with what they already know, so they will be learning how to use an adapted RAN chart to help document that thinking.

3. Show students an image, a book cover, or another visual aid as you tell them the topic they will be reading and learning about in more depth.
4. Ask students to generate ideas about what they think they know about the topic. They can write these down or share with a partner.
5. As a whole group, ask for student responses and document them on the large-format chart so all can see.
6. Ask students if they have any questions or connections about this topic, and add these to the corresponding columns.
7. Tell students that activating prior knowledge and questions is helpful for readers, but strong readers also monitor and revise their thinking during and after reading. Introduce the remaining columns for confirmed knowledge, misconceptions, and new learning.
8. Begin reading the text aloud, and model adding information into the remaining columns.
9. After the initial modeling, ask students to jot down their individual ideas to add to the chart while you read the remainder of the text.
10. Stop periodically to add students' ideas to the chart.
11. The class can continue to add to this chart throughout their learning over the course of the unit.

STRATEGY 2 Anticipation Guide

Anticipation guides include a series of statements related to the topic that students are going to read about or study. The anticipation guide is typically structured to require students to agree or disagree with the statements. Teachers ask students to complete the anticipation guide both before and after reading. The anticipation guide was originally developed by Herber (1978) with a purpose of increasing students' comprehension of a text by actively involving them in making predictions about the concepts in the text. Originally, this strategy was used with secondary students, but more recently it has been adapted to support learners of all ages.

Anticipation guides can take on various forms. The first is primarily informational, where the anticipation guide includes statements outside of common knowledge on the topic of study. Students respond to these statements, providing an initial assessment about their knowledge prior to the reading or unit. Then, students revisit the same questions after reading or the unit concludes to assess their learning. (See Figure 2.3 and see OR 2–2 in the Online Resources for a blank version.) Depending on the language proficiency needs of your students, possible modifications include simplified language, translated anticipation guides, and modified or alternative text.

In addition to connecting to students' background knowledge and experiences, the statements can also serve as a catalyst for discussion about students' beliefs. To get to these thoughtful conversations, the teacher must design statements for the anticipation guide that will effectively elicit conversations that move beyond literal-level

Write A if you agree with the statement.

Write D if you disagree with the statement.

Response Before Lesson	Topic: Rainforest	Response After Lesson
	The rainforest has three layers.	
	Most animals in the rainforest live in the canopy.	
	More than half the world's animals live in the rainforest.	
	There are rainforests on every continent.	
	The size of rainforests is increasing.	
	Toucans cannot fly.	
	Jaguars are an endangered species in the Amazon.	

FIGURE 2.3 *Anticipation Guide* OR 2–2

knowledge. Duffelmeyer (1994) identified four attributes associated with effective anticipation guide statements:

1. Effective statements convey a sense of the major ideas students will encounter.
2. Effective statements activate and draw upon students' prior experiences.
3. Effective statements are general rather than specific.
4. Effective statements challenge students' beliefs.

In the example in Figure 2.4, the unit content is the same, but the statements are designed to elicit both content knowledge and students' beliefs. The goal would be to elicit deeper conversations grounded in beliefs, ethics, and broader systemic issues.

Write A if you agree with the statement.

Write D if you disagree with the statement.

Response Before Lesson	Topic: Rainforest	Response After Lesson
	The rainforest is threatened by illegal logging, mining, and agriculture.	
	Animals will adapt to deforestation.	
	It is worth clearing and destroying parts of the rainforest because it will create new jobs and make money.	
	Climate change is a threat to rainforests.	
	Conservation efforts have little impact on preserving the rainforest.	
	Deforestation and human activities have no significant impact on the rainforest ecosystem.	
	The government should do something to protect endangered species.	

FIGURE 2.4 *Anticipation Guide for Deeper Conversation*

Steps for instruction

1. Identify the type of anticipation guide you want to use (purely informational or one that includes beliefs for deeper conversations).
2. Generate statements for the anticipation guide based on the content the students will be learning during the reading and unit.
3. Tell students you will be starting a new unit and they will complete the anticipation guide at the beginning and end of the unit.
4. Ask students to complete the "Response Before Lesson" section of the anticipation guide and then discuss in pairs or small groups.
5. After the completion of the unit, ask students to complete the "Response After Lesson" section of the anticipation guide and then discuss in pairs or small groups.
6. As a class, discuss ideas that remained the same and ideas that changed over the course of the unit.

STRATEGY 3 Multimedia Preview and Preparation

As noted in the research section, it is easier to learn something new when we can connect it to something we already know. The prereading knowledge-activation experiences in the previous two strategies largely rely on students' prior knowledge without teaching content. However, teachers will often need to support background building prior to having students jump right into the grade-level reading and content. Preparatory texts have been a common recommendation for building confidence and background to prepare students for challenging content. One recommendation has been to provide a simple preparatory text at a lower Lexile® level prior to having students read the more complex texts and topics.

While preparatory texts can be helpful, I prefer multimedia or multimodal previews for multilingual students because they can draw on multiple modes or representations for making meaning. Multimodal presentations of essential information can help students connect to their previous knowledge while simultaneously acquiring foundational concepts needed for the upcoming learning experiences.

The multimedia preview and preparation can take on many forms, such as a related video, slideshow, photograph, newscast, interview, or music. These should include engaging and interesting multimodal content related to the key ideas and concepts that will be part of the upcoming learning. Subtitles or information in students' home language can be helpful for supporting multilingual students, and I also always add an opportunity for discussion around their noticings and reactions to the content.

Steps for instruction

1. Identify key concepts you want to preview to help prepare students.
2. Search online for appropriate videos or resources. There are many online resources for this type of content, but more recently I have been using artificial intelligence (AI) to refine my search by grade level, content, and length. Obviously, you need to watch the content and make sure it is what you need, but it can be a helpful source for narrowing down a search.
3. Explain that the multimedia preview will provide information and help prepare them for the content they will be learning.
4. Share the multimedia preview with students prior to grade-level reading and learning.
5. Ask students what they noticed, what they found interesting, and how it connects to what they already know about this topic.

STRATEGY 4 Making Connections

Proficient readers make connections while they read that help them better understand the text. These might include connections to their own lives or experiences, to other texts they have read, and to events or happenings around the world. While many readers intuitively make connections while they are reading, many students need explicit instruction about how to make connections before, during, and after reading. The classic comprehension strategy of making connections (text-to-text, text-to-self, and text-to-world) became popular and was used in many literacy classrooms after the release of *Strategies That Work* (Harvey and Goudvis 2000). Teachers modeled the strategies by reading a text and documenting their connections on sticky notes or in a reading notebook. Then they prompted the students to document their connections while reading and then share them with a partner or small group.

This comprehension strategy can be beneficial for all learners, but it is particularly helpful for students learning an additional language. It provides time and opportunities to document how students are connecting what they are reading to their prior knowledge and experiences. However, I have also seen some confusion and challenges with teaching this strategy when working with multilingual students. For example, after a teacher and I taught this strategy to a group of second graders, the students thought they needed to use a sticky and write down a connection for anything that was familiar. We had a lot of responses like "There is a tree in the book. There is a tree outside," or "They live in a house, and I live in a house." As a way to encourage students to move beyond superficial use of identification and connection, we created an anchor chart with visuals to talk about the purpose of the strategy, modeled how to make a connection with language frames, and encouraged deeper connections.

Steps for instruction

1. Create an anchor chart that has the outline of the making connections strategy (see Figure 2.5).
2. Introduce the anchor chart and add visual representations for key concepts to help reinforce understanding. For example, you could sketch a picture of yourself for the text-to-self connections and draw a picture of a book for the text-to-text connections.
3. Introduce two options for sentence stems to serve as a language scaffold for multilingual students to document their connections.

Students do not have to use this language, but it is a resource if they want or need it.

4. Begin reading aloud a book and model documenting two connections, one surface-level connection and one deeper connection. Examples might include something like the following: "When I

Making Connections

Purpose: Making connections helps us better understand and remember what we read.

Types of Connections

Text-to-Self: Connection to my life

Text-to-Text: Connection to another book

Text-to-World: Connection to the world

This reminds me of ______________________________________.

When I read ____________________, it reminded me of ______________________________________.

Surface	Deeper
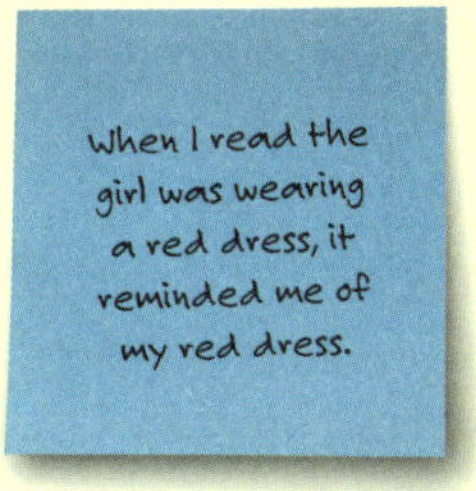 When I read the girl was wearing a red dress, it reminded me of my red dress.	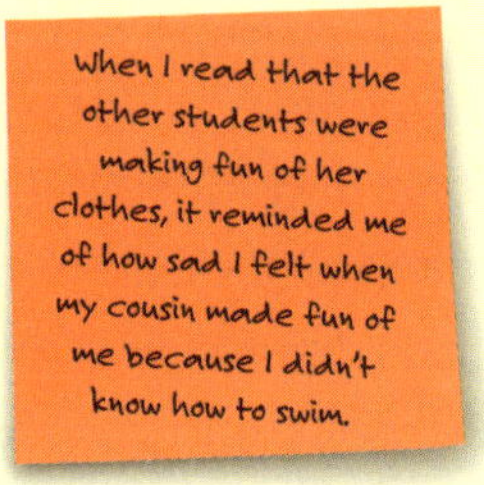 When I read that the other students were making fun of her clothes, it reminded me of how sad I felt when my cousin made fun of me because I didn't know how to swim.

FIGURE 2.5 *Making Connections Anchor Chart*

read the girl was wearing a red dress, it reminded me of my red dress" and "When I read that the other students were making fun of her clothes, it reminded me of how sad I felt when my cousin made fun of me because I didn't know how to swim."

5. Ask students to help you decide in which column you should place each connection.
6. Remind students that the purposes of making connections are to deepen their understanding and help them remember what happened in the text. Deeper connections are the most helpful, so encourage them to document only deeper connections.
7. Ask students to try documenting multiple connections during their reading.

STRATEGY 5 Getting to Know Your Students Through Asset Mapping

While this strategy might seem obvious, getting to know more about your students throughout the year can result in stronger relationships and opportunities for building on students' interests and knowledge outside of school. Most teachers do some initial icebreakers at the beginning of the year where they gather basic information such as how to pronounce students' names, their ages, the languages they speak, their home context, their favorite book or author, and their interests. This is a great start, but our relationships and our knowledge about our students should remain a focus and get deeper over time.

There are many ways to do this, including asking students to write personal narratives or autobiographies, participate in a passion project (where you dedicate research, reading, and writing time in school for studying a topic of interest), or create a multimedia presentation of the assets and resources in their local community. Another option could be creating surveys or reflection opportunities for students to discuss their skills and community practices outside of school.

The funds of knowledge theory (Gonzalez, Moll, and Amanti 2005), as mentioned in the research section earlier, builds on the idea that people are competent and knowledgeable. This knowledge and competency come from many community and cultural resources beyond traditional academic content taught in classrooms. The possibilities for classroom applications and connections are endless when we know more about the strengths and resources in the communities in which we teach. The strategy of asset mapping is a learning experience for teachers and students. Originally used in community planning and for connecting community members, this can also be adapted for learning about and building on students' and the community's funds of knowledge.

Steps for instruction

1. Define the boundary of the community. This will depend on where you live and the age of your students (the entire city, within a ten-mile radius, within a four-block radius, within the school district, etc.).
2. Show a map with the boundary or outline.
3. Decide on the community assets you want to explore with students. Typically we include the following to examine in the community:
    a. Physical assets or world (can be natural or man-made, such as playgrounds, public spaces, facilities, gardens, bike paths, parks, or parking garages)
    b. People assets (skills, knowledge, talent, etc.)
    c. Social networks (informal social networks such as clubs or locally based organizations)
    d. Institutional assets (hospitals, childcare, church, library, school, fire department, etc.)
    e. Economic (business) assets (businesses, such as home businesses, catering, food trucks, and swap meets)
    f. Cultural assets, stories, and heritage (local history, community histories, traditions, community displays of art, sculpture, or dedication, etc.)
4. Brainstorm initial knowledge related to the identified assets and document it in a chart or graphic organizer.
5. Divide students into groups and assign each group an asset.

6. Ask students to document their knowledge and conduct research online to gain information about their assets.
7. Homework for the week will include students talking with at least two community members (could be family or someone outside the home) who can help them learn more about the community asset they are researching.
8. Also do the homework yourself and have one idea to add to each asset.

Assets					
Physical	**People**	**Social**	**Institutional**	**Economic**	**Cultural**
canal park 1 (for kids) park 2 (for pickleball) Arizona Falls bike path on canal	teachers firefighters businesspeople artists engineers doctors nurses landscapers pastors waiters chefs	soccer club Girl Scouts	urgent care school fire department orthodontist animal hospital art center (small, in a house)	coffee shop nail salon frozen yogurt shop convenience store restaurants bank HVAC service	history of citrus groves with irrigation from the canal

FIGURE 2.6 *Community Assets*

9. Together you can create a poster or small mural with visual and textual representations of the community assets.
10. Typically, there will not be enough room to include all the identified assets, so students can choose which ones to include on the visual map.

One class identified the assets within a two-mile radius of their school (see Figure 2.6) and created the map in Figure 2.7.

FIGURE 2.7 *Community Assets Map*

Strategies in Action: Intermediate-Grade Multimedia Preview and Preparation

I was working with Cat Frayne, a third-grade teacher at the Columbus School in Medellín, Colombia. All of her students spoke Spanish at home and were learning English at school. We wanted to build students' excitement about reading while also giving them an authentic purpose for summarizing, so we decided to have book previews every Friday. Students would select their favorite book they read during the week and give an enticing preview of the text without giving away the ending to a small group of their friends. Then, their friends might select that book for their independent reading the following week.

We had to first introduce the key components of a book preview: introduce the book, highlight and summarize key and exciting points of the book, and do not give away the ending. We knew the students had background knowledge about a popular action movie sequel that was coming out that weekend because they had been talking about it in class. We built on this knowledge and interest to introduce the key components of a preview that might entice viewers or, in our case, readers. We showed students the movie preview they had been discussing in class and asked them to help us identify the information in this movie preview that might entice someone to watch it. We watched the movie preview again and together generated a list of what was included: title, characters, setting, summary of the story up to the problem, just enough info to leave you wanting more.

Building from the multimedia preview and background knowledge activation, we told them they would be doing something

Book Preview

1. I read ____ by ____.
2. Tell a little about the book up until the problem
   - First
   - Next
   - Then

★ DO NOT give away the ending!

3. You will love this book because _____.

FIGURE 2.8 *Book Preview Anchor Chart* OR 2-3

similar on Fridays, but with books to recommend to their friends. Together we made an anchor chart to help students prepare for their upcoming book previews. See Figure 2.8 (see also OR 2–3 in the Online Resources).

REFLECTION QUESTIONS

1. What are some ways you currently get to know your students at the beginning of the year?
2. How might you continue getting to know your community, your students, and their background knowledge, interests, and experiences over the course of the year?
3. How could one of these strategies support your multilingual students in an upcoming lesson?
4. What adjustments could you make to one of these strategies to better meet the linguistic needs of your students? Think of multiple versions or modifications that you could use within the context of one strategy.
5. Can you think of areas outside of literacy instruction where one of these strategies would be helpful for your multilingual students?

Teach Academic Vocabulary

VIGNETTE

Briana, a second-grade teacher, came to our coaching and planning professional development session in tears. She said, "I know they can do it. They have been reading and talking about character traits and development. We have been practicing and they have been doing it, but they completely failed the assessment." Another teacher on the team said the same thing happened in her class, and they looked at the third teacher to confirm she saw the same thing with her students, but she did not. Because I knew they had all been planning together and using the same resources, I asked what the third teacher thought helped her students be successful. The third teacher said:

> *During the last assessment, I felt like my kids knew the content and had been successful in class, but it seemed like they didn't understand the language used in the directions and questions. I had been using simplified language to try to help make accessing the content easier for my beginning speakers, but then they would get to the test and not even know what they were being asked to do. So, in this unit I started using the more formal language right from the beginning. I had to support it—give synonyms and examples—but*

I wrote and used words and phrases like elaborate, describe, explain, background knowledge, inference, *and* provide supporting evidence, *instead of language like* tell me, tell me more, how do you know, *and* why do you think that. *And I think it really helped!*

What Does the Research Say?

Teachers often associate academic vocabulary with scientific or content-related terms such as *bioluminescence, plate tectonics, pollen,* and *electrons*. While these are all examples of academic vocabulary, academic vocabulary also includes any language needed to learn effectively in schools. As seen in the opening vignette, students also need the language of academic processes to be successful. Words like *summarize, describe, elaborate, details, evidence,* and *infer* are all crucial academic vocabulary related to literacy, particularly for helping multilingual students show what they know on assessments.

Researchers have documented the importance of academic vocabulary in multilingual students' academic success (August, Fenner, and Snyder 2014). However, this type of vocabulary is much more difficult to learn than social vocabulary, which students hear on a daily basis across multiple settings. Teaching academic vocabulary is a highly effective scaffold for supporting multilinguals in educational contexts (Lesaux et al. 2010). Specifically, instructional strategies should include "using engaging informational texts as a platform for intensive vocabulary instruction; choosing a small set of academic vocabulary words for in-depth instruction; teaching vocabulary in depth using multiple modalities (writing, listening, and speaking)" as well as teaching students word-learning strategies that they can use independently to understand the meanings of words (Baker et al. 2014, 6). Marzano and Pickering (2005) report that effective academic vocabulary instruction includes the following:

- introducing the vocabulary with a definition or description and an example (an image when possible)

- asking students to rephrase the definition in their own words
- asking students to construct a picture, symbol, or representation
- engaging students in activities to add to their knowledge of the word
- periodically asking students to discuss terms or play games related to the terms

The instructional strategies throughout this chapter draw on these research findings.

Five Instructional Strategies

Academic vocabulary plays a crucial role in the educational success of multilingual learners. All the instructional strategies in this chapter include ideas for introducing and supporting retention of academic vocabulary. These activities should be used to engage learners and encourage their independent use of new vocabulary.

STRATEGY 1 Semantic Mapping with the Frayer Model

Semantic mapping is a common and simple instructional strategy we can use to teach and reinforce academic vocabulary. Semantic maps are maps, webs, or visual representations of words that help show the meaning-based connections between words or concepts. Using semantic maps as a teaching strategy has been documented to support multilinguals' ability to understand and recall meanings of words (Udaya 2021).

The Frayer Model (Frayer, Frederick, and Klausmeier 1969) is the semantic map I see used most frequently in multilingual classrooms. The original Frayer Model includes a graphic organizer with four squares for components related to the word: definition, characteristics, examples, and nonexamples. An oval with the focal word is in the center. There are multiple instructional uses for this tool:

1. An instructional strategy to teach the meaning of a word
2. A collaborative instructional activity to complete with students while teaching a word or documenting the meaning of a new word

3. A strategy for students to explore and document their meaning-based understandings of new words

Some teachers have students keep a Frayer Model notebook or dictionary as a way to document their academic vocabulary learning. Teachers have made many modifications of this semantic map. For use with multilingual students, it can be helpful to include a visual representation and students' first language. Figure 3.1 is a modified version used in a Frayer Model notebook (see also OR 3–1 in the Online Resources).

Matt Hajdun, from the Columbus School in Medellín, Colombia, uses the color-coded translanguaging version shown in Figure 3.2 (see also OR 3–2 in the Online Resources). In this version, blue signals the use of Spanish and green for English. If the teacher is preselecting the words, they can write the word in English (in green) and Spanish (in blue) in the center box and leave the other four boxes to be completed by students.

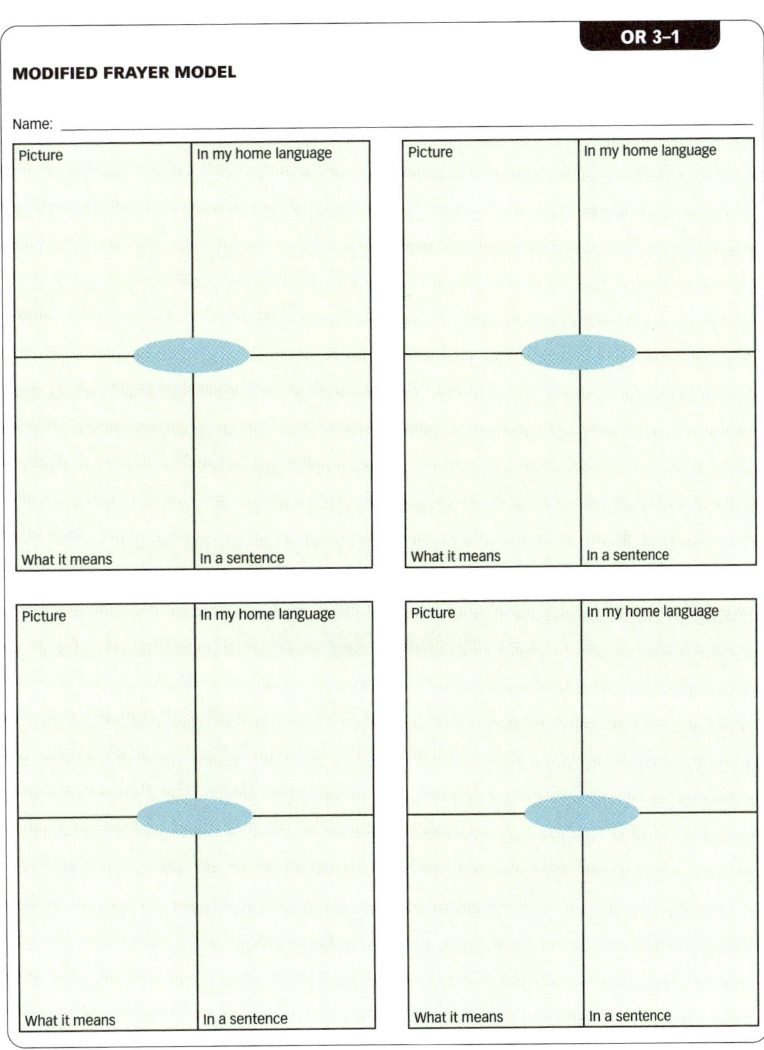

FIGURE 3.1 *Modified Frayer Model Notebook Page* **OR 3–1**

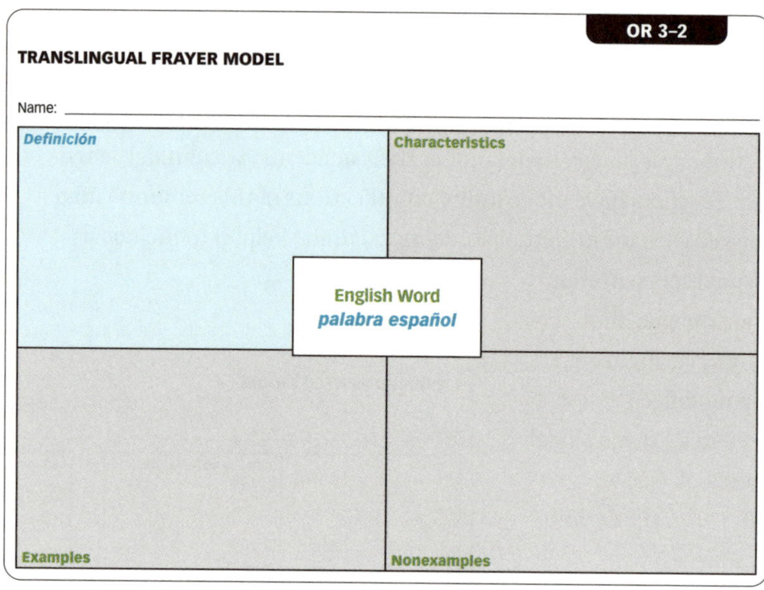

FIGURE 3.2 *Translingual Frayer Model* OR 3-2

The students will write the definition in Spanish (blue), and they will complete the remaining components (characteristics, examples, and nonexamples) in English (green). Or, if the students are self-selecting vocabulary, the students will write the word in English (green) and Spanish (blue) in the center box.

STRATEGY 2 List-Group-Label

List-group-label is a brainstorming instructional strategy teachers can use to build background knowledge, review and reinforce word meanings, or assess students' understanding of a concept and related academic vocabulary. Taba (1967) originally wrote about this strategy as an introductory activity for a unit or lesson to activate prior knowledge about the concept and introduce and categorize related vocabulary with the following steps.

Steps for instruction

1. Identify the key concept or big idea for the unit, lesson, or reading.
2. Ask students to brainstorm a list of all the words they know related to the key concept, and write them on the board or somewhere that all students can see.
3. Have students work in small groups to organize the words from the list into categories. They can also eliminate words or set them to the side if they do not fit into the categories. Encourage students to explain their reasoning for the categorization.
4. Ask groups to label the categories of words and share their categories with the class.

I love this strategy but find it is more beneficial when I make modifications for supporting multilingual learners. In addition to building on background knowledge, multilingual students benefit from seeing visual supports, having vocabulary introductions, reading vocabulary in context, and experiencing repeated exposure to vocabulary. Because of this, I use an expanded version of this strategy before, during, and after instruction with multilingual scaffolds. The following steps provide an outline for a multilingual scaffolded version of list-group-label.

Steps for instruction

1. Identify the key concept or big idea for the unit, lesson, or reading and five to seven academic vocabulary words you think might be unfamiliar to your multilingual students but are essential to understanding the concept.
2. Create vocabulary cards for these words with accompanying images.
3. Ask students to work in small groups to brainstorm a list of all the words they know related to the key concept. They will write each word on a large index card with a quick sketch or visual representation.

4. Have students explain and place their word cards with sketches on the board so the whole class can view the words. Take approximately ten words, depending on age and language proficiency level.
5. Introduce the five to seven preselected academic vocabulary words, if they were not introduced by the students. Give each word, share a brief definition, and show the accompanying image.
6. Encourage students to think about the vocabulary on the board or any new important vocabulary they encounter as you read the text aloud or have students read in pairs or independently.
7. Have students work in small groups to add any new word cards they deem important with sketches.
8. Hand out a graphic organizer for sorting and categorizing the list of words, such as the one in Figure 3.3. (See also OR 3–3 in the Online Resources.)
9. Have students work in small groups to organize the

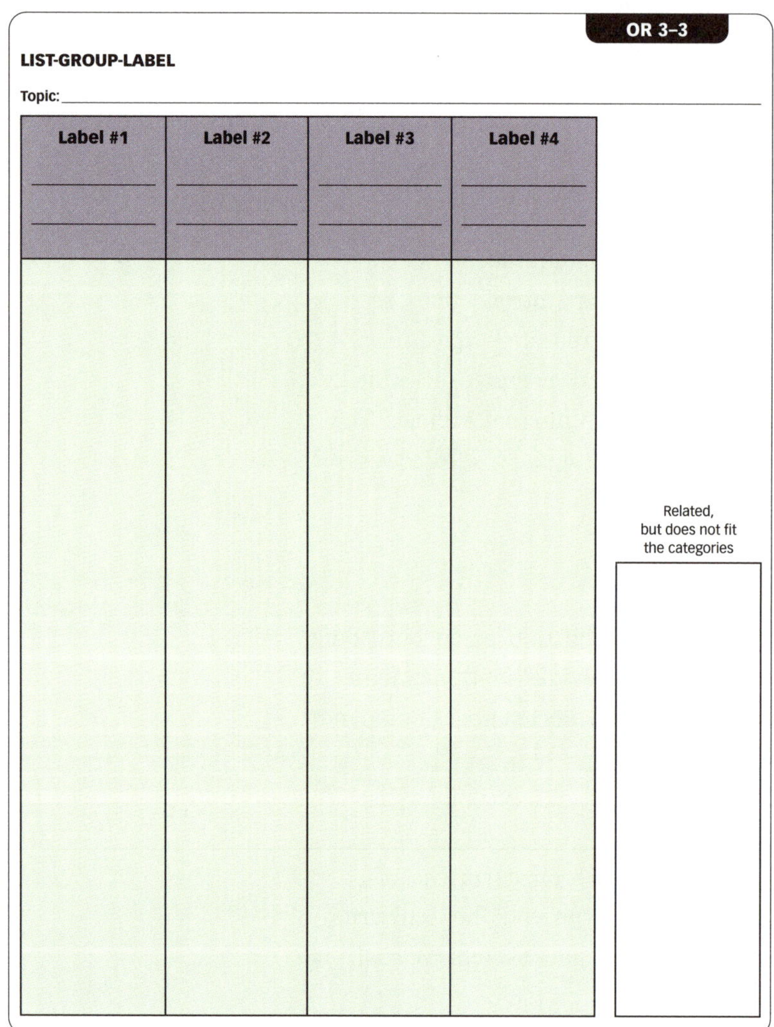

FIGURE 3.3 *List-Group-Label* OR 3–3

words from the class list on the board into categories. Encourage students to explain their reasoning for the categorization.

10. Ask groups to label the categories of words and share their categories with the class.

STRATEGY 3 Heads Up! Academic Vocabulary Version

You have probably seen or played the game Heads Up!, where players try to guess the word on their head from their partner's or teammates' descriptions.

This instructional strategy is a modification of that game that we can use to reinforce and deepen academic vocabulary development in a fun and engaging way. I play this game only with vocabulary that has been previously introduced. I regularly create vocabulary cards with words and images on them to support students throughout both individual lessons and entire units. However, it is important that students see these words on more than one occasion and across time. Playing games to revisit vocabulary can be a fun way to increase retention of these important words, and unlike memory or matching games, where the answers are created for the students, this game requires students to generate descriptions in their own words.

To prepare the materials for the game, print academic vocabulary you have previously introduced on cardstock and cut individual words into cards about the size of an index card. Depending on the age and language proficiency levels of students this could range from ten to thirty words. Make enough copies for distributing to small groups. It is helpful to print the words on dark, thick paper with light ink so that students cannot see through the paper. I use my cards throughout the year and for multiple years, so I laminate them to extend their usability.

Steps for playing the game

1. Divide students into small groups of four or five.
2. The focal student places the stack of vocabulary cards face down in front of them.

3. The teacher starts a thirty-second timer.
4. The focal student grabs a card and lifts it to their head so that the other group members can see it but they cannot.
5. The group members start giving clues to help the focal student guess the word. They can use gestures, give related words (synonyms or antonyms), and describe the word, but they cannot spell it or say things like, "It starts with . . ." or "It rhymes with . . ." The descriptions must relate to content or meaning.
6. Once the focal student guesses the word, they repeat steps 4 and 5 until the thirty-second timer buzzes. *Note:* The focal student has one pass option per round of game play, so if they are stuck on a word, they can say, "Pass," and go to the next word.
7. The group tallies up the number of words the student correctly identified.
8. Repeat steps 2–7 with all members in the small group.
9. The group can add up their collaborative score and set a goal of how much they want to increase that score the next time they play.

STRATEGY 4 Morphological Analysis

When students' morphological awareness increases, they are able to read and understand novel and challenging words. This results in improved reading achievement (Carlisle 2003). This improvement has also been seen with multilingual students (Kieffer and Lesaux 2008). Multilingual students who received instruction on morphological analysis strategies significantly outperformed peers who did not (Davidson and O'Connor 2019).

Morphemes are the smallest units of meaning or grammatical function used to create words (Yule 2010). Morphemes consist of base or root words, prefixes, and suffixes. For example, *teachable* contains two morphemes (the verb *teach*, "to assist in learning how to do something," and the suffix *-able*, "able to"), which can be combined to mean "able to be taught." Another example, *teaching*, also contains two morphemes, *teach* and *-ing*. The *-ing* morpheme forms the present participle of the verb *teach*.

There is a wide range of complexity levels related to morphological analysis. I begin by telling my multilingual learners that I think learning about root words, prefixes, and suffixes is similar to getting cheat codes for the English language. Once we understand them individually and how they can work together, it unlocks the meanings of so many new words!

Using a base-and-suffix matrix is a simple instructional strategy for introducing morphological analysis. I typically start with a familiar word and morphemes to help them get familiar with the process before moving on to more challenging ones. I also always try to connect this to words we see in context, as opposed to just rote memorization. I specifically select words from a text we read together to use as examples in the matrix. I then also encourage students to continue to look for similar words and patterns that we could analyze in the matrix to help them connect how morphological analysis supports their real-life reading experiences. Following are instruction options for morphological analysis at three levels of complexity.

Steps for instruction

1. Create and display the matrix.
2. Select a noun from a book you are reading or have recently read together to add to the matrix, for example, *cat*, and read the word aloud. Write it in the left side of the matrix. (See Figure 3.4.)

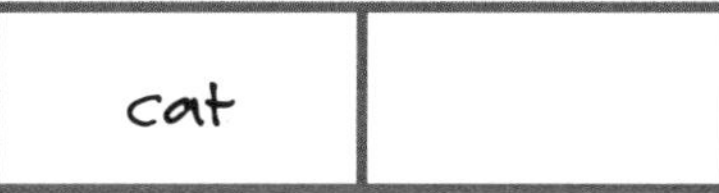

FIGURE 3.4 *Matrix with Base Word*

3. Ask students what the word would be if there were more than one cat. If needed, prompt them with context such as, "I have one cat; Sally has two . . ."
4. Ask students what they need to add to the end of the word if there is more than one cat.
5. Add the *s* into the right side of the matrix. (See Figure 3.5.)

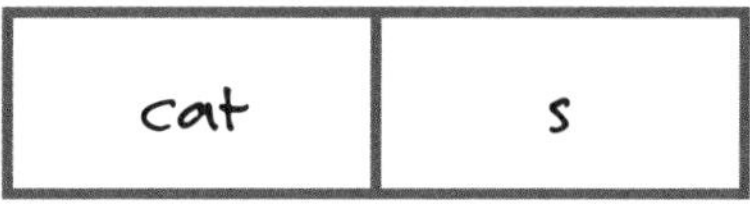

FIGURE 3.5 *Matrix with Base Word and Suffix*

6. Tell students that the base word is *cat* (point to the box and tell them this is where the base words go in the matrix), and the *s* is a suffix. Ask them to talk to a partner about why you

added *-s* to this noun to reinforce that it changes the meaning to be plural (more than one).

7. Repeat with a few new words.
8. Have students generate some words and add the plural suffixes.
9. Give students examples of plural words from the book and have them segment them into the appropriate base and suffix boxes.

After students understand the basic matrix, move on to a more sophisticated one that includes columns for prefixes, base words, and suffixes (see Figure 3.6). Start with a familiar word the first time you use the new matrix. In subsequent sessions, you can introduce new and more complex morphemes or use the matrix to analyze new words you encounter while reading.

Steps for instruction

1. Identify a base word that will have many options in the morphological family.
2. Place the base word in the middle box.
3. Ask students to talk with partners to come up with as many words as possible with the base word.
4. Ask them to share out their ideas, and document them in the matrix.
5. Ask students to discuss in pairs how each prefix and suffix changes the meaning of the base word. (See Figure 3.6.)

Prefix	Base Word	Suffix
re	play	ing ful s ed er

FIGURE 3.6 *Morphology Matrix*

As students become more proficient with morphological analysis, they can begin to document their analysis when they are reading and working independently. This independent practice helps reinforce the morphological strategies used to decipher and understand unknown words. Figure 3.7 (Wisconsin Department of Public Instruction n.d.) is a semantic map that students can use independently when reading complex texts (see also OR 3–4 in the Online Resources).

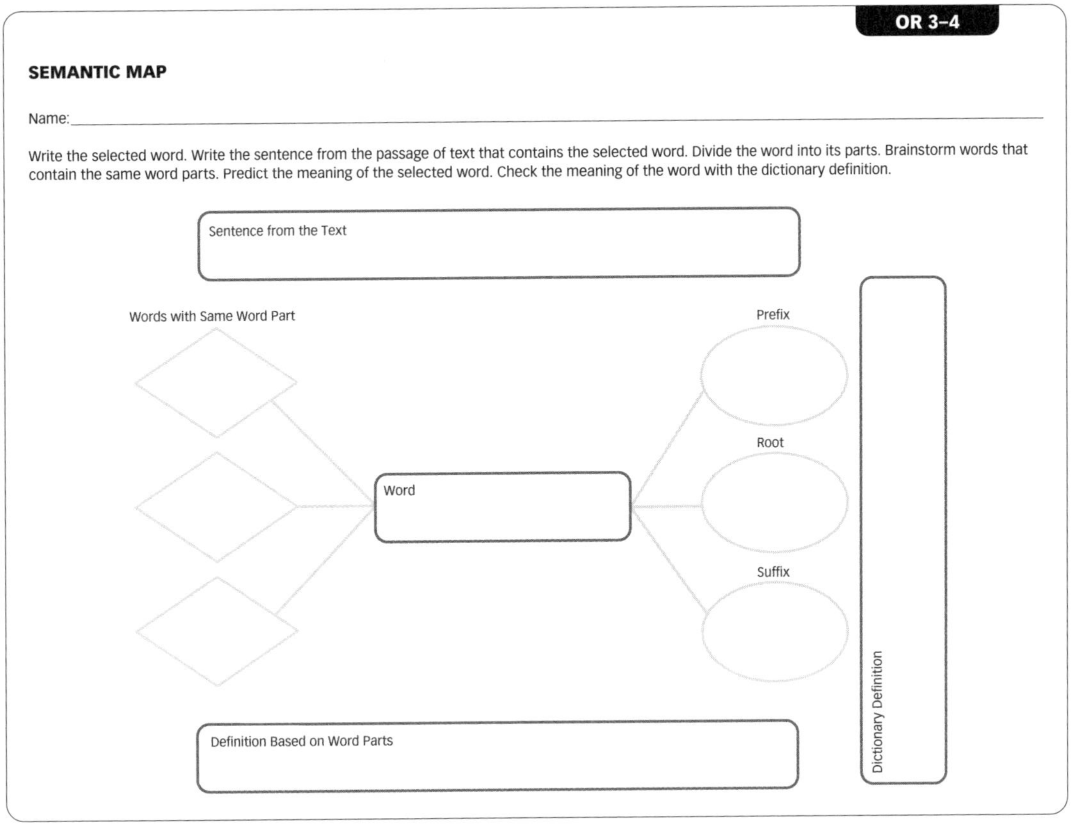

OR 3–4

SEMANTIC MAP

Name:________________________________

Write the selected word. Write the sentence from the passage of text that contains the selected word. Divide the word into its parts. Brainstorm words that contain the same word parts. Predict the meaning of the selected word. Check the meaning of the word with the dictionary definition.

Sentence from the Text

Words with Same Word Part

Prefix

Root

Word

Suffix

Dictionary Definition

Definition Based on Word Parts

FIGURE 3.7 *Semantic Map* **OR 3–4**

STRATEGY 5 Partner-Practice-Place-Defend

Partner-practice-place-defend is an instructional strategy I created to support academic vocabulary development through instruction, repeated exposure, and opportunities for practice and rehearsal. I typically use this strategy when we are working with informational text and I want students to understand vocabulary deeply in context and relation to other connected vocabulary words. Topics like volcanoes, the solar system, and habitats are all great topics to use for this because you want students to learn the vocabulary words that are all related and connected in one context. Then, the students will use images and labels of the vocabulary to create a visually representative word wall.

Steps for preteaching

1. Select seven to ten key academic vocabulary words that will be crucial to the content learning and reading of the text.
2. Create vocabulary cards with an image, the word, and a definition or description.
3. Briefly introduce the word cards to the students prior to reading aloud the text.
4. Draw attention to the vocabulary when reading the text aloud.
5. Revisit the vocabulary cards and ask students to take turns with their partners stating the meaning of the vocabulary in their own words.

Steps for instruction

1. You will need to have the following prepared: images or illustrations of the vocabulary words, individual labels (written vocabulary words), and a poster with a sketch of whatever the environment or context is that you are studying (for example, the outline of a volcano, as shown in Figure 3.8).
2. Display the poster on the wall and give each student one card with an image or a label on it (see examples in Figures 3.9 and 3.10).

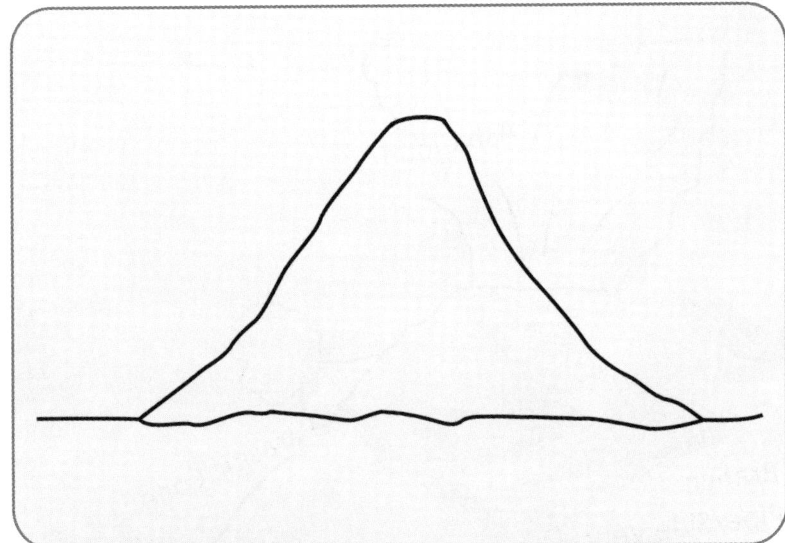

FIGURE 3.8 *Volcano Outline*

FIGURE 3.9 *Parasitic Cone Sketch*

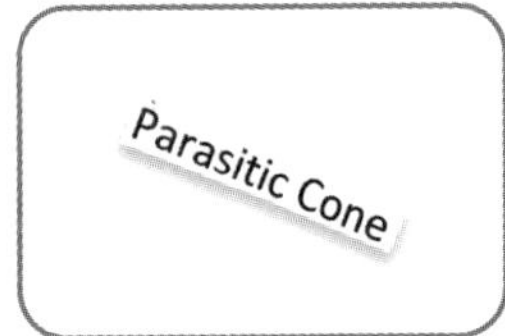

FIGURE 3.10 *Parasitic Cone Label*

3. *Partner:* Students move around the room silently with their image or label and try to find their partner (that is, they match images with labels to form partnerships).
4. *Practice:* Students discuss with their partners where their image and label would go on the larger context (poster). They practice what they are going to say when they place the word in context. They must use the vocabulary word in a sentence and include supporting evidence to explain why they are placing it in that location. For example, a student might say, "When magma comes out of the earth, it is called lava. So we are putting the lava outside the volcano."
5. *Place:* Students place the image and label on the poster one at a time.
6. *Defend:* Students provide supporting evidence, defending why they placed the vocabulary word where they did.
7. Keep the poster on the wall as a point of reference throughout the unit to support academic vocabulary usage (see the example in Figure 3.11).

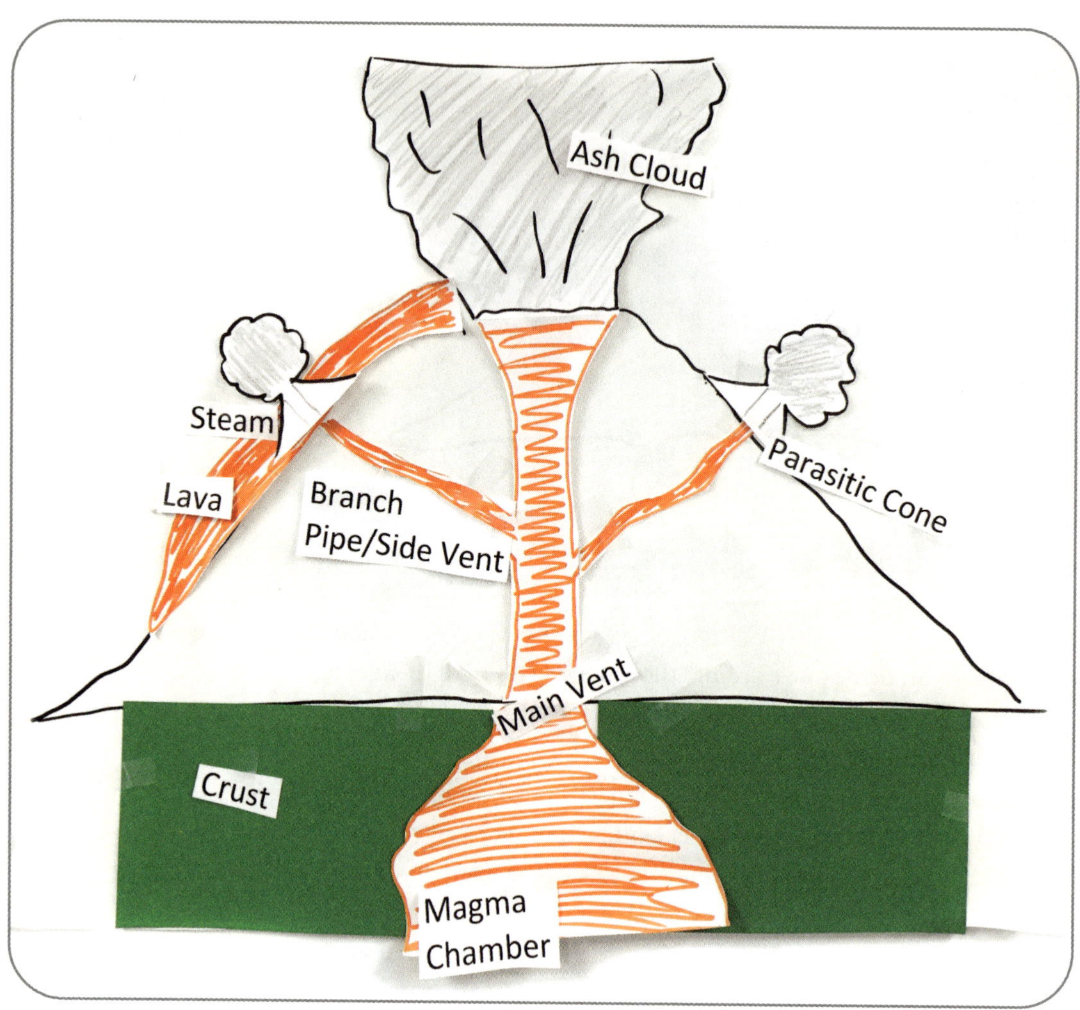

FIGURE 3.11 *Volcano Poster*

Strategies in Action: Primary-Grade Modified Bilingual List-Group-Label

Rachel, a second-grade bilingual teacher, decided to combine her science unit on the rainforest with her informational reading and writing unit. She knew the vocabulary would be challenging, so she wanted to provide as many exposures as possible to reading, writing, speaking, and listening related to the rainforest. She decided to start the unit with the list-group-label strategy to build background knowledge and get a sense of what students knew about the rainforest. Because she taught in a bilingual setting and her students were still in the beginning stages of learning English, she modified this strategy to include bilingual listing, grouping, and labeling. She believed that students had background knowledge about the rainforest but may not have been exposed to this academic vocabulary in English yet.

Rachel created bilingual vocabulary cards for the following words because she knew students would encounter them in the reading frequently and they were essential to understanding core concepts about the rainforest: *emergent layer, canopy layer, understory layer, forest floor, habitat,* and *humid*. Rachel displayed a large picture of the rainforest on the board with the bilingual title "Rainforest/Selva." She asked the students to work in their table groups to brainstorm a bilingual list of all the words they knew related to the rainforest. She gave them three minutes to generate the list. Then, she asked each table group to give her two vocabulary words with translations, and she wrote them on the board. Each group had to add two words with translations that were not yet added by a previous group. The students came up with the following list, which she added to the board: *toucan/tucán, snakes/serpientes, monkeys/monos, rain/lluvia, trees/árboles, bugs/insectos, frogs/ranas, forest/bosque, sloth/perezoso.*

Rachel told them this was a great start, and she wanted to add a couple of more words that she thought they needed to know and would see in the reading. She then added her bilingual vocabulary cards to the board while giving a brief definition and adding an image to each.

Rachel told the students they were going to read a short informational book in English about the rainforest with their reading partners. She encouraged them to add to their list if they found new vocabulary words they thought were important. After reading, the students added three additional words: *flora, fauna,* and *dense*. Rachel gave them the list-group-label graphic organizer, and most groups came up with the categories of animals, weather, and layers. However, the fourth categories and words that did not fit differed by group. Rachel told the students they would be learning many new words related to the rainforest throughout this unit and they would do the list-group-label activity at the end and compare it with their knowledge right now to see how much they had learned. This would be a great way for Rachel and the students to reflect on their learning.

REFLECTION QUESTIONS

1. How are you currently teaching and supporting the development of academic vocabulary?
2. What academic vocabulary is currently most challenging for your students?
3. How might you apply one or more of these strategies in your upcoming lesson or unit?
4. How could you modify, like Rachel did, one of these strategies to better meet the linguistic needs of your current students' language proficiency levels?
5. How might you integrate more opportunities for practicing and reinforcing academic language?

Model Skills, Strategies, and Procedures

VIGNETTE

Nataliya, a recently resettled fifth grader from Ukraine, was terrified to go to her new school and begged her mother to let her stay home. Her mother reassured her that she would love it, just like she loved school in Ukraine. She reminded her daughter that she was a top student last year in school and she would be again here in the United States. Nataliya pleaded with her mom in Ukrainian to let her stay at home until she learned more English. She told her mom that she wouldn't have any idea what was going on in school because she knew only a few words and phrases in English, and she feared the students would laugh at her. Her mother reassured her it would be fine.

Nataliya arrived at school, and to her surprise, her teacher, Mr. Jones, had created a welcome packet for her. In her packet, Mr. Jones included a series of visual resources for Nataliya to better understand the classroom and to communicate with visuals when she needed something. He created a visual schedule with times and pictures of what they did during each time of day. Mr. Jones also created documents of common procedures accompanied by images or sketches, like the one in Figure 4.1 (page 52). The final documents in the package included visual representations with sentences to communicate basic needs such as requesting to go to the bathroom, needing a drink of water, not feeling well, and feeling confused or needing help. He modeled holding these up or placing them on top of her desk to signal she needed something. Mr. Jones also gave Nataliya a tablet to use in the classroom with a translation app downloaded and showed her how to use it.

Nataliya was so thankful to Mr. Jones. His thoughtful preparation not only allowed her to understand and participate in the common procedures of the classroom but also signaled that he understood and cared about her schooling experience.

What Does the Research Say?

Nataliya's fear is common for many students entering a new school system and learning a new language. This can be increasingly challenging for newcomers who are in the intermediate grades because they may have experienced previous academic success. The content and language are quite sophisticated by the intermediate grades, so it can feel stressful and embarrassing to not yet understand simple classroom procedures and conversations. Thoughtful modeling of skills, strategies, and procedures can reduce multilingual students' anxiety and increase their opportunities for learning and participation.

While modeling and strategy instruction have been widely accepted as quality literacy instruction with monolingual students (National Reading Panel 2000), the effects of that same comprehension instruction on students learning English are not the same (August and Shanahan 2006; Saunders and Goldenberg 2007). Multilingual students need additional support to access grade-level content. Modeling, making instructions and learning tasks clear by providing comprehensible input and reinforcement (visual cues and gestures), providing options for repeated practice, and providing language supports, like sentence stems, all support multilingual students' ability to participate in learning and documenting what they know (Echevarria, Vogt, and Short 2007; Echevarria, Short, and Powers 2006).

The instructional strategies throughout this chapter draw on these research findings.

Five Instructional Strategies

Modeling is part of daily instructional practice when teaching children new academic skills. However, modeling for multilingual learners should also include strategies and procedures necessary for being successful in the classroom. In this chapter, I share five instructional strategies that support multilingual students whose proficiency ranges from the very beginning stages to nearly proficient.

STRATEGY 1 Model Classroom Procedures

Modeling classroom procedures and expectations is an important part of any smoothly running classroom. However, for students newly learning English, a spoken or written explanation of what to do for classroom routines may not provide enough support for them to understand and remember the expectations. These may seem like simple tasks, but it can feel overwhelming to students when they don't understand the "simple" parts of learning and routines. Feeling successful with the common procedures and expectations sets the primary foundation for feeling safe and ready to learn. Physical modeling, visual schedules, and routines documents with supporting images can be helpful for students.

Steps for schedules

1. Identify the weekly and daily schedules, including specialized instructional time outside the primary classroom.
2. Take photographs of where and what each part of the schedule looks like. Ideally, take photographs of your actual classroom. If that is not possible, you can find images online to use.
3. Display the daily schedule. It is helpful if you don't just show it once in the morning but rather make it visible throughout the

entire day. I recommend creating and laminating a poster for each day of the week or using a pocket chart and adjusting it daily.

4. For as long as needed in the beginning of the year, when a new student comes, or a new schedule is introduced, refer to the visual schedule and physically model where students will be going. Practice going to the locations with students.

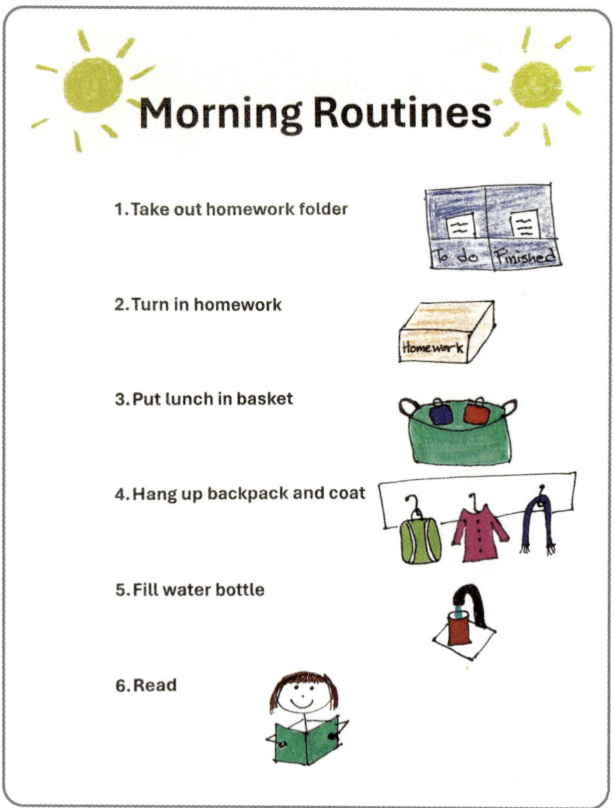

FIGURE 4.1 *Routines*

Steps for classroom routines

1. Identify the common routines students will complete on a daily basis. The most common might be start- and end-of-day routines.
2. Create a document with visuals and simple language for the steps.
3. Show students the steps and model the steps.
4. Ask students to complete the steps independently.
5. Display the steps in an appropriate area (you might place morning routines near where students hang their backpacks and jackets, for example).
6. Some teachers like to make this into a laminated checklist on students' desks so they can check it off each morning.

Figure 4.1 is similar to the visual routines document mentioned in the opening vignette.

STRATEGY 2 Model Academic Procedures

In the previous strategy, I discussed the basics of modeling classroom schedules and routines. Those procedures are essential and repeated on a regular basis, but students also receive procedural instructions multiple times a day about how to complete academic tasks in order to participate in learning experiences and document what they know. The academic language used in instructions can feel daunting for multilingual students, and multistep procedures can be difficult to remember, especially if students are uncertain about some of the language. Modeling and using clearly identified steps to complete the academic procedures help set multilingual students up for success.

Steps for instruction

1. Identify the steps for the academic procedure.
2. Create an anchor chart, slide, or large-print format of the step-by-step procedures.
3. Introduce the anchor chart or document to students and model each step with examples from classroom learning.
4. Ask students to help you come up with a visual representation to add to each of the procedure steps.
5. Ask students to talk with a partner to review what they will be doing step-by-step, taking turns. Encourage them to ask any questions or clarify expectations.
6. Leave the chart displayed throughout the lesson.
7. Five minutes before the activity ends, encourage students to revisit the steps to see what they might need to add or change.
8. Have students talk with a partner about what they accomplished in each step.

FIGURE 4.2 *Partner Reading Expectations*

Small-group learning experiences are often independent if students are not in the small group with the teacher. I like to create a visual document similar to the morning routines, but for expectations of the group, and place it in the small-group location. For example, see the expectations for the partner reading corner in Figure 4.2.

As an alternative, students can create their own academic procedures models, like the example in Figure 4.3.

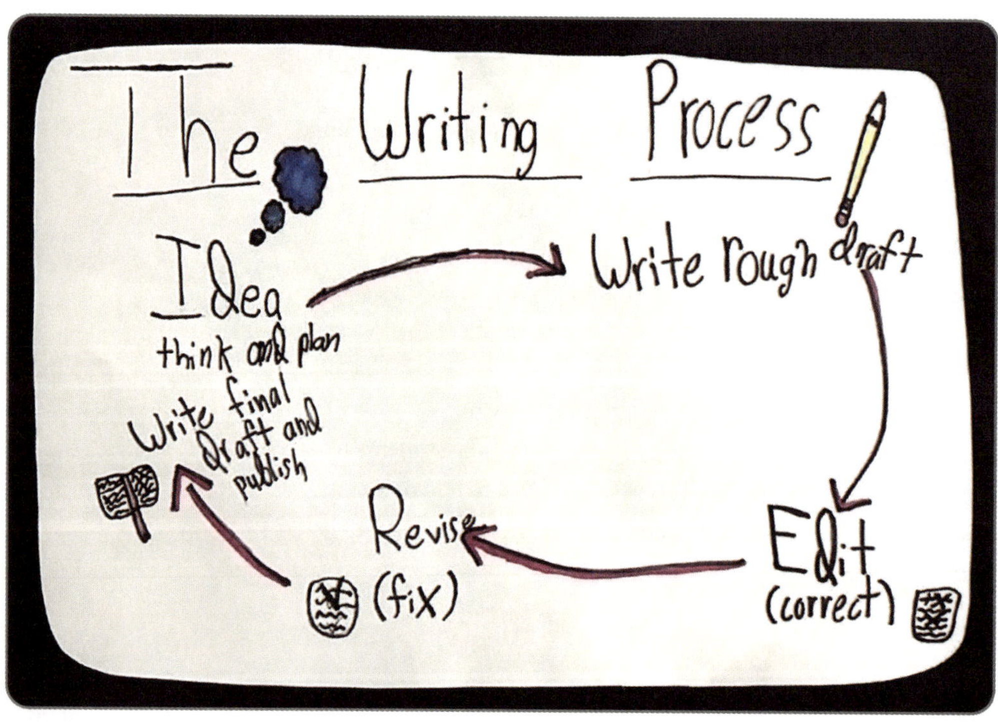

FIGURE 4.3 *Writing Process*

STRATEGY 3 Model Reading Strategies

Many research studies have documented the importance and effectiveness of teaching students comprehension strategies (Duke and Pearson 2009; Shanahan et al. 2010). While much of this research focused on monolingual students, this work is helpful for multilingual students also. Teachers often initially model these comprehension strategies using think-alouds during a whole-class read-aloud. Think-alouds are a wonderful strategy but can be difficult for multilingual students to comprehend if their only resources for modeling are oral language from the teacher. When I introduce a reading strategy, I always try to model the strategy with an accompanying anchor chart that includes visuals, the purpose of the strategy, highlighted academic vocabulary, and a sentence stem to document the use of the strategy. This helps students understand when and for what purposes they might use the strategy, reinforces the academic vocabulary they might encounter on assignments and assessments, and helps build expanded, full-sentence responses. See Figure 4.4 for an example.

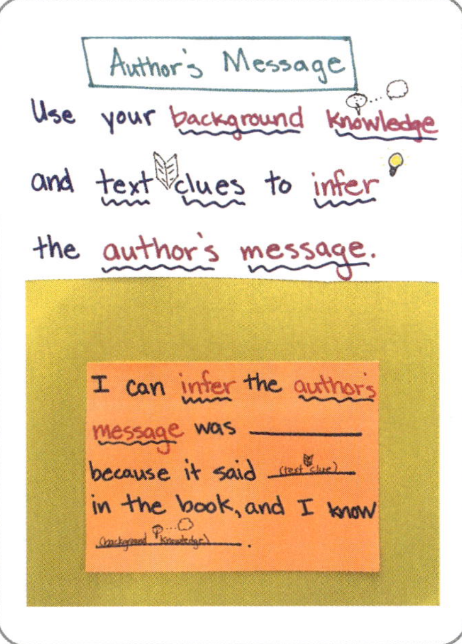

FIGURE 4.4 *Author's Message Anchor Chart*

Steps for instruction

1. Identify the strategy and its purpose.
2. Create an anchor chart that includes the following:
   a. Strategy name
   b. Purpose
   c. Highlighted academic vocabulary
   d. Visuals
   e. Sentence stem for documenting strategy
   f. Example
3. Model using the strategy during a read-aloud.
4. Encourage students to try using the strategy with a partner.

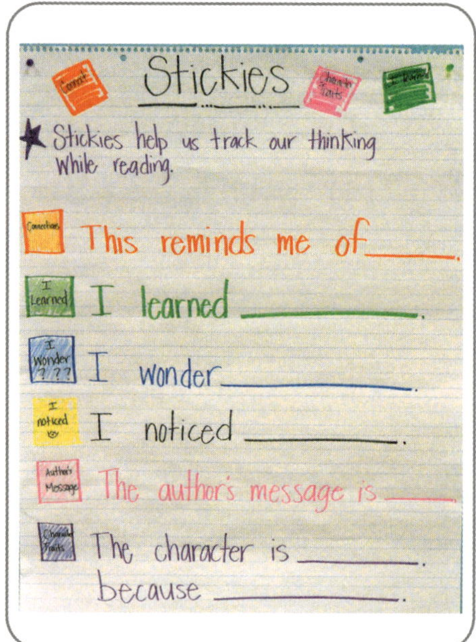

FIGURE 4.5 *Strategies Anchor Chart*

5. Encourage students to try using the strategy independently and documenting it on a sticky note or in their reading response notebook.

One additional but important thing to note about strategy and skill development is that it should be ongoing. If we are teaching students a skill or strategy that's used by proficient readers, then we want to make sure they understand that it will be part of their reading repertoire long beyond the week when we introduce the strategy. Too often I see students thinking these strategies are something they use only when prompted by their teacher during the week it was introduced.

To remedy that misconception and remind students that strategies are used at different times and for different purposes depending on what they are reading, we created an anchor chart that included all the previously introduced strategies, shown in Figure 4.5. To support multilingual students, we color-coded the strategies and included a sentence stem they could use with each strategy. Students could then choose which ones to use during their independent reading and place in their reading response notebook at the end of the week.

STRATEGY 4 Model Giving Feedback

Giving feedback can be a challenge for all students, but it is also a great opportunity to reflect on expectations and learning, use oral language for academic conversations, and support peers. I recommend modeling and practicing two types of feedback: (1) generalized feedback that students can use across learning outputs and (2) specific, detailed feedback related to requirements of a larger single learning output.

Begin feedback modeling early in the year to create a classroom community that is comfortable with giving and receiving feedback.

Establish the parameters of the feedback including using kind language and providing supportive feedback that will enhance future learning. Remind students that feedback is not about right or wrong, and authors are the ultimate authority of their work and do not have to make suggested changes if they so choose.

Steps for generalized feedback

1. Create a rubric for generalized feedback such as the one in Figure 4.6 that includes sentence stems (see also OR 4–1 in the Online Resources).
2. Create a sample assignment that is missing a component.
3. Explain to students that they will be regularly giving feedback to partners and in their groups, so you want to practice what that looks like.
4. Show them the rubric and explain it.
5. Model how you would give feedback on the sample assignment you created.

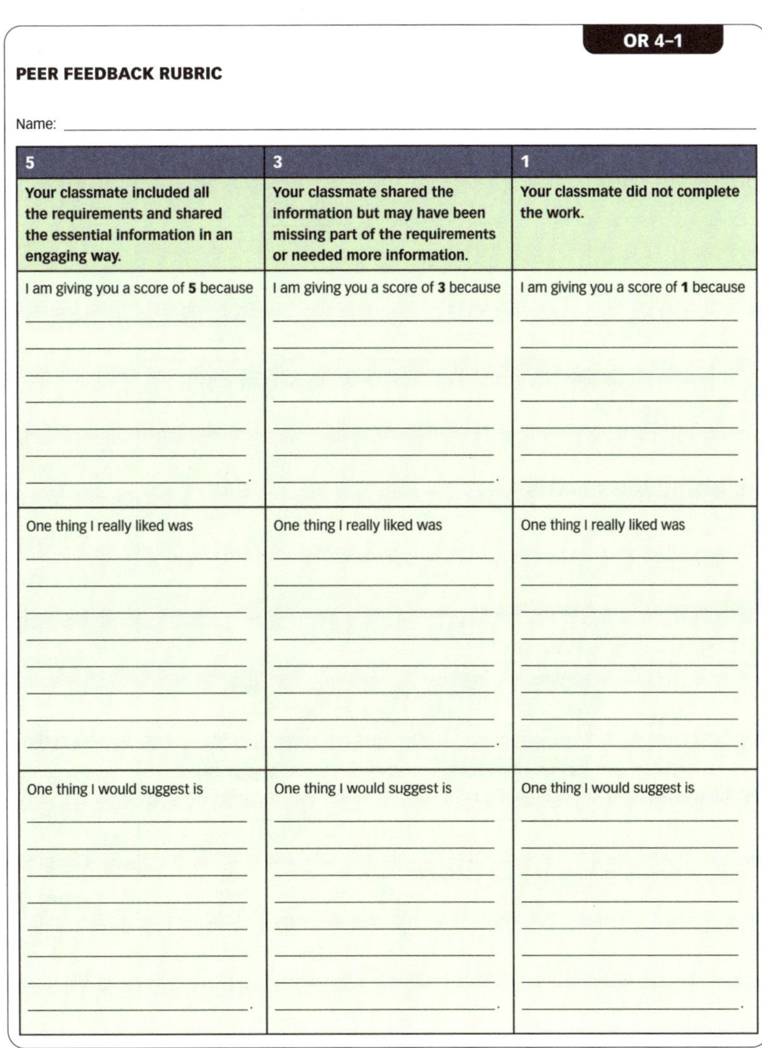

OR 4–1

PEER FEEDBACK RUBRIC

Name: ______________________

5	3	1
Your classmate included all the requirements and shared the essential information in an engaging way.	**Your classmate shared the information but may have been missing part of the requirements or needed more information.**	**Your classmate did not complete the work.**
I am giving you a score of **5** because ______________________.	I am giving you a score of **3** because ______________________.	I am giving you a score of **1** because ______________________.
One thing I really liked was ______________________.	One thing I really liked was ______________________.	One thing I really liked was ______________________.
One thing I would suggest is ______________________.	One thing I would suggest is ______________________.	One thing I would suggest is ______________________.

FIGURE 4.6 *Peer Feedback Rubric* **OR 4–1**

6. Ask students to try giving feedback to each other after completing their next assignment.
7. Have the students refer to the rubric often. They can use this generalized feedback form on nearly any student output.

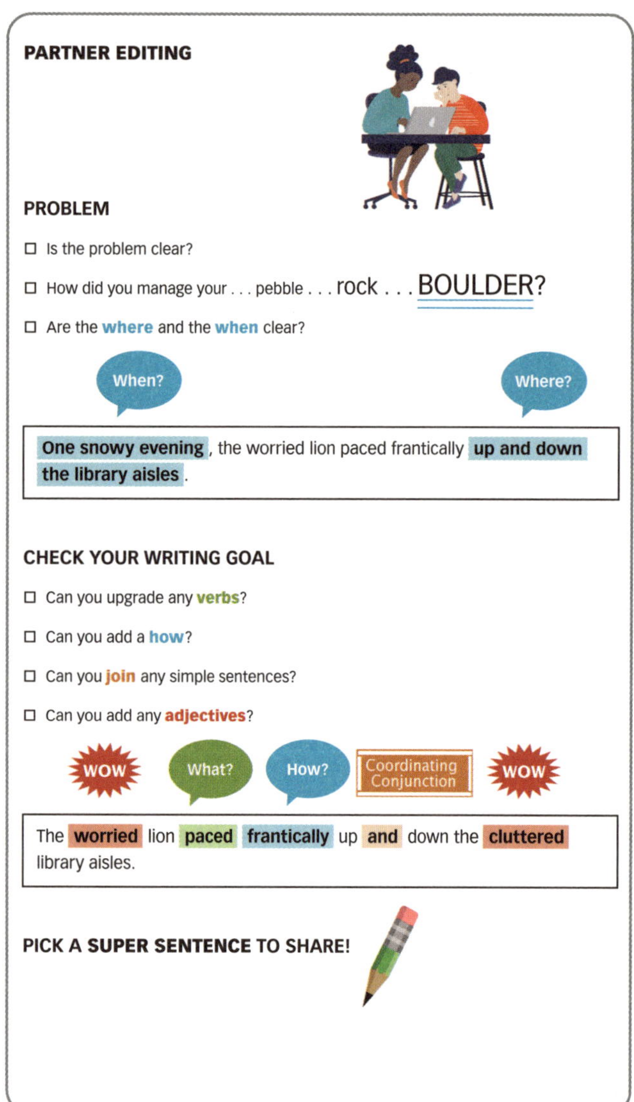

FIGURE 4.7 *Partner Editing Checklist*

Steps for specific and detailed feedback

1. Design rubrics and feedback guidelines for a specific assignment that are directly related to the steps and requirements you will introduce while modeling the assignment and giving instructions.
2. Create a checklist with questions to ask students related to the instructional concepts previously introduced.

Include visuals and examples when possible. See an adaptation of Tam's example in Figure 4.7. In this checklist, Tam included key aspects that had been emphasized during instruction. This included writing a clear problem that builds from a small problem (pebble) to a slightly larger problem (rock) to the biggest problem and climax of the story (boulder). It also included an emphasis on their own personalized writing goals.

STRATEGY 5 Model Degrees of Proficiency for Student Critique

Sometimes the most helpful way to model for students includes presenting them with examples of varying degrees of proficiency. When the teacher always models a perfect or ideal version of writing, reading, responses, or other assignments, it can be difficult to understand the nuances of what makes a response mediocre or outstanding. Likewise, a mere description of what makes the assignment outstanding might feel abstract to students or include unfamiliar language. Presenting students with three versions of the same piece of writing and asking them to critique the work allows them to identify and discuss the aspects of writing that make certain pieces of writing better than others. This can also help students think about how they might make their own work stronger.

Student critique of multiple versions of a concept can be used in almost any context. When talking about fluency, I frequently ask students to think about what would be the necessary qualities for people to get hired to read audiobooks. I then model a slow and halted style of speaking, and students tell me I need to read faster. Then, I read like an auctioneer, then completely in monotone, and finally with expression and fluency. I ask the students to not only discuss which one was better but also identify why and what characteristics they would want to emulate when reading aloud.

The most common model and critique I have seen teachers use is for writing. It provides a concrete way for students to see different types of writing strengths and areas of support in many areas including voice, structure, details and elaboration, syntax, and editing. Here I describe the steps for how to do this with writing, but you could adjust it for any content area or assignment.

Steps for instruction

1. Identify the goals and outcomes for the assignment. Ideally, you have already created a rubric or have a rubric to use with student-friendly language.

2. Generate student-friendly examples at three levels of proficiency that you would expect to see from students in this age range (try to avoid just two levels in order to model multiple components of the task).
   a. If it is a multifaceted assignment, such as writing, make sure to include identifiable examples of each aspect in the top-tier level. In the next levels, purposefully demonstrate less proficiency in those aspects.
   b. Some curricular materials or assessment materials may already have student examples for various levels or scores on rubrics, so those could also be helpful resources.
3. Share the rubric with students and explain that they will be evaluating three pieces of writing and then discussing their evaluation with peers.
4. Provide language to support critique with evidence, such as "I believe the paper deserves a [score] in the category of [category from rubric] because [supporting evidence that connects rubric criteria and what is in the paper]."
5. Give students time to read the examples independently and take notes on their responses.
6. Have students work in pairs or small groups to discuss. They may adjust their thinking and evidence.
7. Ask groups to share out and discuss agreements and discrepancies.
8. Draw attention to any aspects that were not addressed.
9. Ask students to connect this to their upcoming work.

The example in Figure 4.8 includes a rubric for opinion writing in a first-grade classroom with three examples. These three samples provide a wide range of strengths and needs in the different categories, so they would make a strong choice for modeling degrees of proficiency for student critique. For example, in Sample 1 students would likely identify that the writing scored a 5 in all categories except editing because it had two mistakes. They would then use the language from the steps above to discuss with peers. If there were any misconceptions, the teacher would address them before asking students to evaluate Sample 2.

	5	3	1
Introduction and Stating Opinion	Clearly introduces the topic and states a clear opinion	Introduces topic, but opinion is unclear	Does not have an introduction or does not state the opinion
Supporting Reasons	Provides three or more reasons that clearly support the opinion	Provides two reasons that clearly support the opinion, or provides three reasons, but they do not clearly support the opinion	Provides only one reason to support the opinion
Concluding Statement	Provides a strong concluding statement that reinforces the opinion	Provides a weak concluding statement that does not reinforce the opinion	Does not include a concluding statement
Editing	Includes less than two editing errors	Includes two to five editing errors	Includes more than five editing errors

Sample 1

Students sit next to the same person for the whole day for a long time. Where students sit changes how they feel and how much they learn. That is why Mrs. Gonzales should let students choose their own seats.

Some students are shy, and it is hard for them to talk with people they do not know. If Mrs. Gonzales let students choose their own seats, shy people would feel good and do better working with their friends. The class would be kwieter if students could sit

FIGURE 4.8 *Rubric for Opinion Writing*

continues

continued

next to their friends because they wouldn't have to yell across the room to tell their friend things. Also, friends could help friends sitting next to them make good choyces. Finally, students will learn better if they are not sitting by a person they do not like.

In conclusion, all students will be happier and learn more if they choose their own seats, so Mrs. Gonzales should let students choose their own seat.

Sample 2

Dear Mrs. Gonzales,

Cude you pleas let us chus our sit. Risin one are name takes are falling off alrdy. Risin two sum time it can be lonle wen pepil dont tok to us. So Mrs. Gonzales plese let us chuc are sit.

Love,

Student

Sample 3

We should get to choose our seats because it would be more fun. Mrs. Gonzales please let us choose our seats. I will love you forever and bring you a gift if we can choose our seats. I would like to sit next to Augustine. We are best friends. We will be good.

FIGURE 4.8 *Rubric for Opinion Writing*

Strategies in Action: Primary-Grade Expanded Modeling of Procedures

Rachel was teaching second grade in a bilingual school where all of the students were newly learning English. She was modeling and teaching how to complete self-selected research and inquiry projects. Rachel knew students needed reinforcement on the skills and procedures, so she first introduced their objectives (see Figure 4.9) to help students get a broad overview of what they would be doing, why they would be doing it, and how they would know they had done it.

Next, Rachel introduced a synthesizing and summarizing strategy and modeled how to do the process using a book they had been reading as a whole class. As seen in Figure 4.10, she gave step-by-step directions and provided examples to help students remember. Now that she had introduced the academic skill, Rachel showed them an anchor chart titled "I'm Ready to Show My Learning." As she introduced each step in the academic procedure students were expected to complete, she asked students to help her create a visual to remind them what to do.

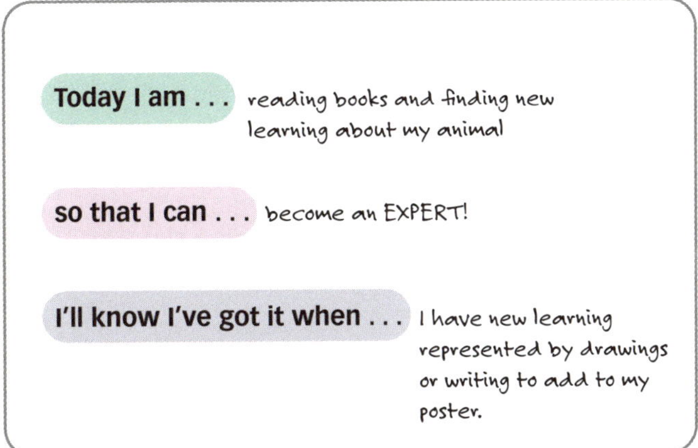

FIGURE 4.9 *Procedures*

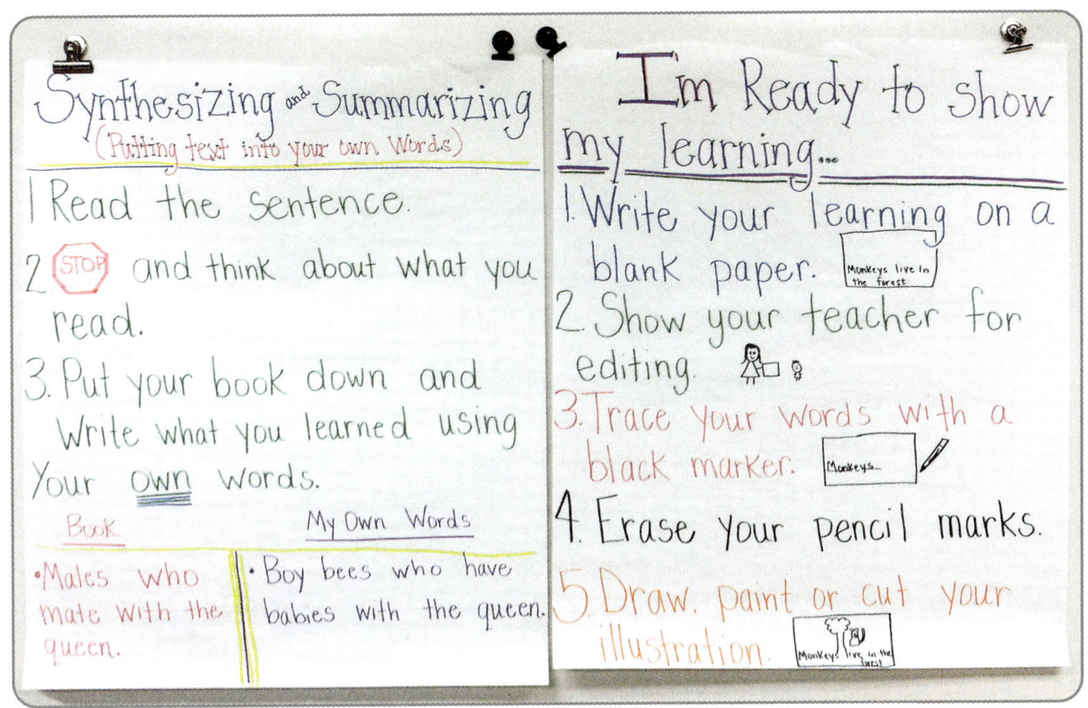

FIGURE 4.10 *Synthesizing and Summarizing*

Students then had an opportunity to practice using English with their partners to recall the steps they would complete during the independent work period.

REFLECTION QUESTIONS

1. What successes have you had in the past with modeling skills, strategies, or procedures for multilingual students? What aspects of your modeling helped make this successful?
2. What challenges have you had with supporting multilingual students' understanding of skills, strategies, or procedures?
3. What skill, strategy, or procedure is most needed to support your multilingual students right now?
4. How might you apply one or more of these teaching strategies in your upcoming lesson or unit to support that skill, strategy, or procedure?
5. How could you modify one of these strategies to better meet the linguistic needs of your current students' language proficiency levels?

Use Visuals to Support Understanding

VIGNETTE

I was teaching second grade at a bilingual school in a small community in Colorado. I was teaching in English, and my multilingual students worked so hard and did incredible work during an informational text unit that was part of the required curriculum at the time. However, the postunit test included reading a text-only passage about ports and harbors. It had vocabulary like *freighter, tugboat,* and *ferry* that was completely unfamiliar to most of my students. While my students had learned to synthesize and summarize information from informational reading, they were often reading about familiar topics and could use visuals and text features to support vocabulary development and comprehension when reading. They did not have this in the postassessment, and my multilingual students did not score well. I was frustrated and complained that the assessment was not actually measuring whether or not students had met the literacy-related objectives of the unit—it was measuring the background knowledge and vocabulary about a foreign concept.

I was told that the assessment was not optional. The next year, I asked my principal if I could put five vocabulary words with images from the text on the board (*port, harbor, freighter, tugboat,* and *ferry*). She said I could not provide any instruction or discussion about what they were or read them aloud to the students, but I could tell students that they would encounter these words in the assessment and they could use the images as a reference. We had a significant increase in scores with just five photos with the words below. Because students had some context of what the keywords and title were, they were able to use context clues and background knowledge to infer. For some of my multilingual students, the images made a difference between passing or not passing that assessment.

What Does the Research Say?

Our world is dominated with images, but school contexts often have a focus on text-based comprehension. However, researchers have documented that visual aids increase the effectiveness of teaching a second language (Ilomo and Ilomo 2021). Using visuals to assist in vocabulary learning has been documented as being more effective than using purely text- or oral-based approaches because visuals can help teachers clarify and make learning more concrete (Thomas and Reinders 2010).

Teachers working with multilingual students can use pictures and videos to make connections across languages by providing access to the meaning without having to translate. This also helps multilingual students connect to prior knowledge about a concept, regardless of language proficiency levels (Kang 2004), thus providing the necessary comprehensible input for language learning (Echevarria, Vogt, and Short 2007). Supporting visuals can take on a range of formats, such as photographs, pictures, realia, movies, and gestures.

Five Instructional Strategies

All of the instructional strategies in this chapter include some type of visual representation. Some of the strategies are used by the teacher to help provide access to content and others are strategies students can use to document what they know or support communication. It is common practice to accompany the introduction of a vocabulary word with an image to support multilingual students, but there are many more ways to incorporate visuals than picture vocabulary cards. The following instructional strategies and classroom examples build from the research on using visuals to support understanding.

STRATEGY 1 Visuals for Introducing Vocabulary and Building Background Knowledge

Using visuals such as pictures, videos, and realia is the most common strategy I see teachers using to make content comprehensible for multilingual students. This strategy is simple and effective, and it can mean the difference between a student understanding the gist of the learning or feeling completely confused. This can take on a range of formats: picture vocabulary cards, visual word walls, picture dictionaries, diagrams, realia (actual objects), and videos (with or without captions or translations).

Showing images in slides when presenting vocabulary can be a helpful strategy to introduce new words, but I find students need to be able to see and reference the images more than just during the introduction. Because of this, I recommend creating a longer-lasting format such as an anchor chart, a student handout, or some way for students to document what they are learning with visual support.

For example, I was working with a fourth-grade classroom on a comics and graphic novel genre unit. We wanted students to analyze the author's use of various comic design features. We first asked students to look through the books and talk about what they noticed. We jotted these features down on an anchor chart with the proper terminology and a visual representation, as shown in Figure 5.1. Then we asked students to work with partners to do a visual analysis of these features in a comic. They used sticky notes to document when they found a feature and the purpose they thought it served. After they found two instances of each, they re-created this chart in their writing notebook and filled in the "Purpose" column with a partner. We discussed it as a class, and students had the opportunity to revise their document. They could then add to this dictionary as they encountered new features during reading. We encouraged students to use this when they began their own comic compositions.

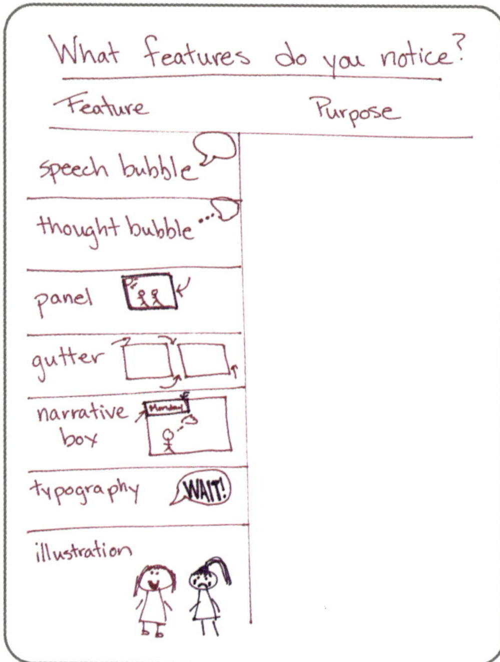

FIGURE 5.1 *Features Anchor Chart*

Steps for instruction

1. Identify essential vocabulary and background knowledge needed for student success.
2. Select a visual representation mode that best suits the learning. For example, a process might best be demonstrated in a video, whereas a strategy such as visualizing might be best presented on an anchor chart with academic vocabulary and visuals.
3. Introduce the visual; reinforce with language.
4. Provide continued access to the visual with accompanying language.
5. Ideally, make it interactive so that students can contribute to it when they apply their learning.
6. Revisit throughout learning and encourage students to use it.

STRATEGY 2 Total Physical Response

Gestures and physical movement or representation help multilingual students learn new words and language and make content comprehensible. Teachers can use gestures and physical movement during instruction, but it is also beneficial for students to participate in the movement. The teacher can act out or make gestures for vocabulary words in the simplest form. For example, giving physical movements to feelings or verbs when teaching singular vocabulary is a common instance of using total physical response (TPR). The teacher might model initially and then encourage the students to act out the words. This can then evolve into phrases and sentences. Eventually students can act out parts of stories or other content the teacher deems appropriate.

I find this approach is most helpful with students in the beginning stages of language learning, but it can be adapted for intermediate levels as well. For example, when wanting to help expand terminology, I could start with *walk*, which all intermediate students would know. Then I could introduce more sophisticated terminology such as *limp, stumble, tiptoe,* and *stagger.* Some teachers play Simon says to help reinforce new language. Other teachers might have students play games like charades for repetition and physical representation of previously taught concepts and language.

This strategy is great because it takes very little preparation and the physical movement helps students make additional mental connections, making retention more likely.

Steps for instruction

1. Identify key vocabulary, phrases, or important concepts that could be represented physically.
2. Model the physical movement while introducing the language.
3. Ask students to participate in the movement while using the language you introduced.
4. Provide opportunities to revisit and practice the physical movements.

STRATEGY 3 Typography That Supports Language Learning

Font, bolded print, underlining, and color-coding can all support multilingual students. These small aspects can help draw attention to important information, signal an instructional focus or part of speech, or help students make cross-linguistic connections. When teaching students parts of speech, many teachers use color-coding as a way to reinforce concepts. For example, one teacher circles the verbs in blue, underlines the nouns in pink, and puts lines around the adjectives. Other teachers underline the first letter of a sentence in green to signal it is the start of the sentence and needs to be capitalized. Then they underline the ending punctuation (or where it should be) in red to signal the completion of the sentence.

There are many ways to use color, underlining, and print to support students. As seen in Figure 5.2, this teacher of students newly learning English used color to help represent the concept and provide visual representation to support students sorting new vocabulary related to hot and cold. Students received pictures and sorted them into the categories hot and cold.

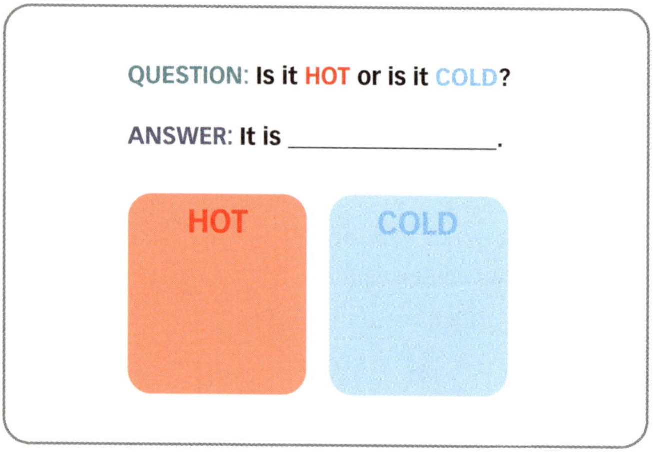

QUESTION: Is it HOT or is it COLD?

ANSWER: It is ______________.

HOT

COLD

FIGURE 5.2 *Hot or Cold*

This strategy is not just for beginning speakers. It can also be used to help build metalinguistic awareness. As seen in Figure 5.3, Cat Frayne created a bilingual word bank with powerful words to use and highlighted cognates across English and Spanish.

Powerful Words
Bilingual Word Bank

powerful	poderoso
best	mejor
should	deberían
definitely	definitivamente
most	máximo
important	importante
terrible	terrible

FIGURE 5.3 *Powerful Words Bilingual Word Bank*

In the anchor chart in Figure 5.4, the teacher used a blue squiggly line to signal academic vocabulary. This teacher wanted to expose students to academic vocabulary, highlight it, and encourage students to use it, so she drew attention to the words with a blue squiggly line in all her anchor charts.

Steps for instruction

1. During lesson planning and preparation, identify key concepts or vocabulary that you could reinforce with typographical choices.
2. Add bold, highlighting, underlining, or color-coding to help teach or reinforce new vocabulary or concepts.
3. Encourage students to use new vocabulary or concepts when appropriate.

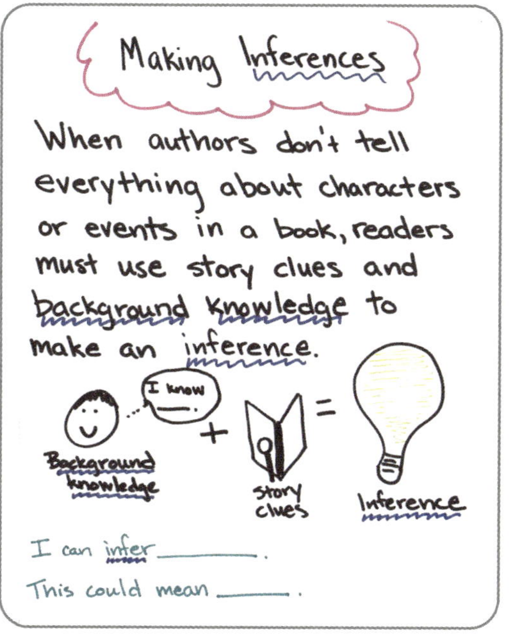

FIGURE 5.4 *Making Inferences*

STRATEGY 4 Multimodal Documentation

There are many ways people access information and document what they know beyond written language. However, written language dominates academic contexts. This is not the way most adults consume information or present information. Typically, they include images, designs, videos, and so on. Australia, for example, has multimodality standards because it is such an important consideration for meaning making and communication in current society.

In schools in the United States, students often read increasingly complex text with decreasing amounts of visuals, and they are most frequently assessed on written products. This makes showing what you know more difficult for multilingual students. Including multiple modes (text, image, video, audio, gesture) for documenting knowledge is a more inclusive practice that allows all students, regardless of language proficiency, to document what they know. Here are five possible multimodal representations to help students document their learning in literacy:

1. *Sketchnotes* are visual notes that use a creative and graphic representation to document and record students' thoughts, reading, or learning. They often include drawings, shapes, visual elements, framing, and handwriting or typographical features as a way to capture understanding. These notes are helpful to document learning but also beneficial to revisit for reinforcement and to study content. Tanny McGregor (2018) has a fantastic educational book on sketchnotes. Figure 5.5 is a sketchnote she made while attending a webinar I gave about supporting multilingual learners in the reading workshop. Such a beautiful way to capture learning! I also often create a sketchnote prior to teaching a lesson or a difficult reading. I then use it as a visual preview for my students to help make the content more comprehensible. Then, they can create their own sketchnotes.

FIGURE 5.5 *Sketchnote*

2. *Infographics* are a collection of visuals and data that present easy-to-understand information (see Figure 5.6). They are frequently used in branding and to make data easily accessible to all readers. Infographics can be a great way for multilingual learners to document what they know about a topic or demonstrate their ability to persuade. Emphasis on graphic representation with powerful but succinct text decreases stress around language proficiency and output so the multilingual students can focus on content.
3. *Illustrated documentation* could be a range of options to allow students to illustrate their responses. This could include illustrating in graphic organizers, responses to questions, and demonstrations of processes.
4. *Video creation* is a great way to integrate technology, content, and language. Video creation also allows multilingual students

FIGURE 5.6 *Waste Recycling Infographic*

opportunities to rerecord, if they are not pleased with an initial attempt. Students can document what they know via a student newscast, documentary, stop-motion piece, puppet show, dramatic performance, and so on. See examples of this work in the "Strategies in Action" section.

5. *Drama* could include experiences such as students reenacting a story they read or using puppets to retell a story.

Steps for instruction

1. Identify student learning objectives.
2. Generate ideas for demonstrating competency in the learning objectives that include various multimodal options.
3. Model multimodal representations. For each type, students will need to see examples, see you model, and have opportunities to practice. These are new skills that have not had nearly the educational focus of text-based products.
4. Encourage students to select a multimodal representation that best serves their needs.

STRATEGY 5 Picture Word Inductive Model

The picture word inductive model was originally developed by Emily Calhoun (1999) to support listening, speaking, reading, and writing. It is now a popular ESL strategy, often referred to as PWIM. It is a fun, interactive learning experience centered on a visual provided by the teacher. In general, the teacher presents a visual and students help collaboratively label the picture. Then, the students create sentences about the picture, building from the labels. This strategy is often spread across multiple days (two to three). There are many variations or ways teachers could modify this strategy depending on the stage of language proficiency and the content focus in their classroom. The following is my adaptation of the PWIM to better support multilingual students. Figure 5.7 is an example of a PWIM I did with students using a photo I took while working with schools in Australia.

KANGAROO

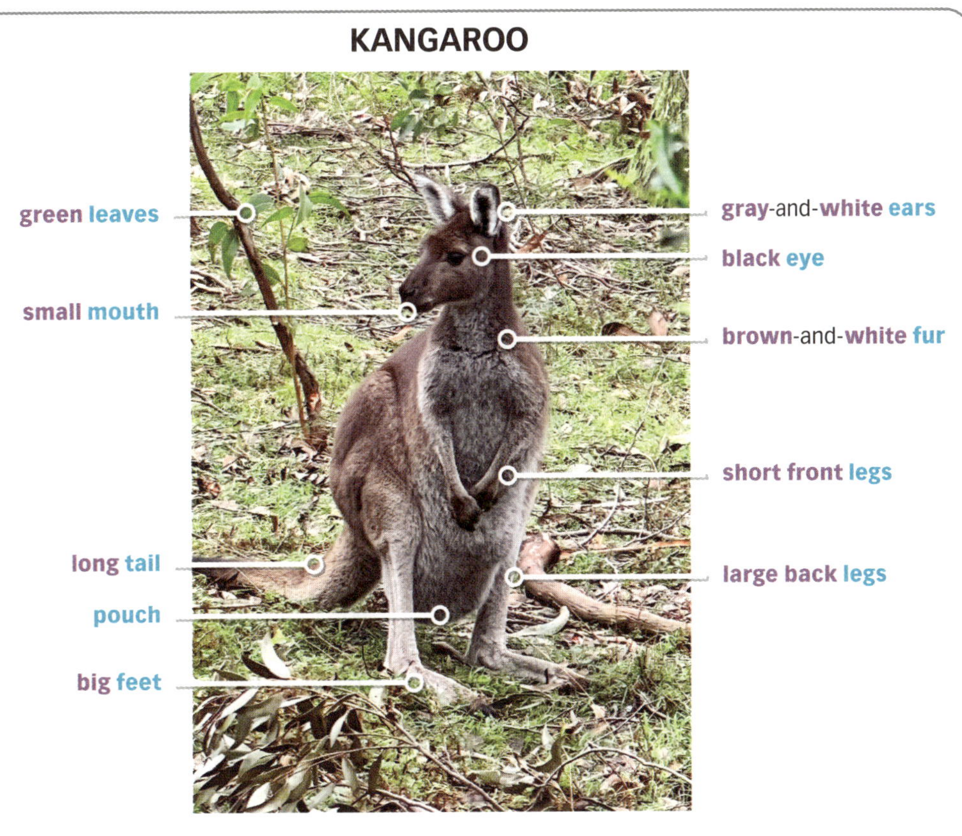

SENTENCE STEMS

The kangaroo has ______________________________.

I see ______________________________.

STUDENT SENTENCES

The kangaroo has gray-and-white ears.

The kangaroo looks at me with his black eye.

I see big feet.

FIGURE 5.7 *PWIM*

Steps for instruction

1. Select a picture and present it to the class, displaying it on the board and giving students a copy.
2. Students talk with partners to generate ideas for words or labels for the picture.
3. As a whole group, students call out words or phrases, and you write them on the board for all students to see. Typically, teachers use color-coding to signal different parts of speech. For example, they write verbs in green, nouns in blue, and adjectives in purple.
4. Revisit the words frequently and have students chorally read and reread the labels.
5. Students get together in partners or small groups to discuss possible titles for the picture and generate sentences about the picture.
6. If needed, provide sentence stems to support the completion of the sentences.
7. The students share ideas with the whole class as you record their ideas on a chart or below the picture.
8. Students chorally read the sentences.
9. Students independently write their own sentences.

Strategies in Action: Primary-Grade Multimodal Documentation

Tam Jarowyj and I were working on a collaborative research project in her second-grade classroom. She had a goal of increasing student engagement and enjoyment during writing. Her students had a wide range of writing abilities, and she wanted her most reluctant writers to engage in meaningful ways of writing, telling, and presenting their stories. Tam created a multimodal narrative writing unit that included planning with a graphic organizer using text or illustrations, orally telling their story, writing their story, and creating a movie of their story. We told the students that they would be having a movie premiere in which the administration would come to watch the release of their movies to create excitement and an intended audience of their multimodal work.

Tam noted that this particular class was motivated by art and more creative modes of representation. Because of this, she decided to have the students create four sets or scenes for the backdrop of their movies. She thought this would inspire their writing by helping them think about details and describe their setting throughout multiple points in the sequence of their story. Figures 5.8 and 5.9 are the first two scenes for the movie and story of a reluctant writer who had previously voiced frustration with the writing process. However, as seen in this image, his detailed and interactive settings helped him think through and articulate the plotline along with extensive details about how a spider hacked Buckingham Palace. He took great pride in his set design, puppet creation, and movie filming and editing. He used his multimodal creation as a reference point that he continually referred to while writing the text-based version of the story that he used to narrate the movie.

FIGURE 5.8 *Scene 1*

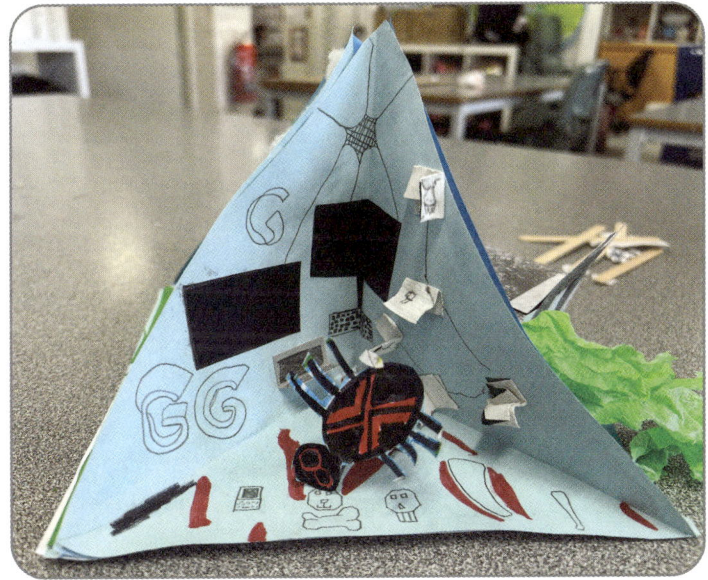

FIGURE 5.9 *Scene 2*

REFLECTION QUESTIONS

1. In what ways have you previously used visuals to support multilingual students?
2. What successes have you experienced with using visuals to support multilingual students?
3. What challenges have you experienced with using visuals to support multilingual students?
4. How might you apply one or more of these strategies in your upcoming lesson or unit to support multilingual students?
5. How could you modify one of these strategies to better meet the linguistic needs of your current students' language proficiency levels?

Adjust Speech and Time

VIGNETTE

I am a Spanish language learner. I took Spanish in high school and a few college-level courses, had a Spanish teaching practicum in my teacher preparation program, and worked as a teacher in a bilingual school (mine was the English-speaking classroom). I never felt confident in my language abilities, so I started one-on-one tutoring two to three days a week for six months before I moved to Medellín, Colombia, for my sabbatical and a research project. I had a brilliant teacher, Sindy, and we spoke primarily in Spanish during our sessions. I was feeling confident as I packed my bags to move to Colombia for a semester.

I went to check in to my apartment rental and had to speak with the portero (doorman) who allows entrance to the apartment building to get my key. The first exchange went smoothly; then he began to give me extensive details at what felt like warp speed. After I missed the first concept, I panicked, and while I was trying to figure it out by translating it in my head, he moved on to three additional topics and posed a question. I felt defeated and overwhelmed as I apologized for my poor Spanish and asked him to slow down and tell me again.

I met with Sindy the next morning for tutoring at a café. The conversation was going well, and I began reflecting on why it felt easy with her, unlike my experience the previous evening. I noticed her slowed speech with clear enunciation, pausing at points to check in with me by rephrasing or asking for my input and clarifying as needed. She did all of this scaffolding and support with oral language in Spanish, but it made a huge difference. Sindy also never seemed impatient when I needed a few extra seconds to process what I was going to say. All of this not only helped with my understanding and ability to communicate but also decreased my anxiety and made me more likely to take risks with language.

What Does the Research Say?

Many researchers have documented the impact of speech rate on comprehension (Flowerdew 1994; Matsuura et al. 2014). As one might expect, slowed speech typically facilitates increased comprehension for people learning a new language (Griffiths 1990; Flowerdew 1994). Much of this research was done by having participants listen to audio at different speeds and assessing their comprehension. More recent research in education has indicated that slowed speech in classroom instruction is an effective scaffold for supporting multilingual students by making content more comprehensible (Echevarria and Vogt 2010; Goldenberg 2013). As my experience with the portero in Colombia proved, speech rate made the difference between understanding one-fifth of what he was saying and understanding all of what he was saying. This is a simple and easy-to-make adjustment that teachers can implement into their instruction immediately without any significant preparation.

Adjusting time is another easy-to-use scaffold requiring minimal preparation. There are multiple simple strategies that teachers can use to facilitate deeper and more meaningful participation and learning experiences for multilingual students. While multiple studies document the benefits of providing wait time (Gambrell 1983; Hindman, Wasik, and Bradley 2018), researchers have also documented the lack of wait time observed in classrooms. In one study, researchers found the overwhelming majority of Head Start teachers in the study waited less than one second for students to respond (Hindman, Wasik, and Bradley 2018). Additional research has documented that adjusting time is an effective practice to meet multilingual students' needs (Echevarria, Vogt, and Short 2007; Yaqubi and Rokni 2012). This could include adjustments in response time, work completion time, time for instruction, and time with direct teacher support. The strategies here build on the research base of adjusting speech and wait time to support multilingual students.

Five Instructional Strategies

The instructional strategies in this chapter often take little to no preparation. Instead, they require only making a conscientious plan and commitment to considering adjusted speech and time needs for multilingual students.

STRATEGY 1 Adjusted Speech Rate Incorporating Videos

As teachers, we often speak quickly as we try to move through content so students can begin working and applying the new learning. However, if students are unable to understand the content and instructions because we move through it too quickly, additional time will be lost because we'll have to repeat the information.

As seen in the vignette, slowed speech with clear enunciation is a simple and effective scaffold to make the content of instruction more comprehensible for multilingual students. Accompanying gestures or visual representations with slowed speech are also helpful. Teachers can easily integrate this into any and all instruction. An alternative option for this strategy includes incorporating more video into instruction. This could include prerecorded instruction from the teacher or professionally created and produced material that students could watch independently prior to applying learning or working with peers. There are multiple benefits for using video with multilingual students, including the opportunities to slow the speed of the video, to pause and rewatch, and to use captions. You are probably familiar with how to slow the speed of a video, but this might be a new tool for your students.

Steps for instruction

1. Provide students with a link to the video.
2. Model the following steps:
   a. Click on the settings icon.
   b. Click on playback speed.
   c. Select a speed.
3. Encourage students to watch at the speed that is most comprehensible for them, and remind them that they can pause and rewind or rewatch when needed.

STRATEGY 2 Extended Wait Time

Processing time is important for all students, but extended wait time is essential for providing opportunities for participation for multilingual students. Students who are in early stages of working toward proficiency in English will often still be translating the teacher's question or prompt in their mind when another student is sharing the answer. Establishing routines of noncompetitive wait time after asking a question allows multilingual students enough time to process and translate and prepare their response without being discouraged by other students answering before they have time to comprehend. The wait time will largely depend on the lowest level of language proficiency in the classroom. You will also want to adjust the wait time depending on how many scaffolds you have for response. For example, the teacher can slightly decrease wait time if they have a sentence stem and the question requires a simple response. Likewise, students will need extended time if the response is open ended with fewer language supports and requires more elaborate language. The following steps provide an easy, low-stress way to begin establishing the amount of wait time needed in a classroom. While teachers do not need to do this for every response, it gives an idea of needed processing time.

Steps for instruction

1. Explain to students that everyone needs different amounts of time to do different things and that thinking and responding is not a race.
2. Share with students that it is distracting when someone is trying to think and the person in front of them shouts out the answer or waves their hand in the air.
3. Explain that you are going to ask students a question and you want them to raise a thumb to their chest when they are ready to respond. This physical movement is much less distracting than raised hands.
4. Wait until all students have a thumb to their chest.

STRATEGY 3 Adjusted Time to Complete Tasks

As mentioned in the previous strategy, processing time and completing tasks take different students different amounts of time. For multilingual students, particularly in the beginning stages of proficiency, completing reading and writing tasks can take significantly longer because of the time needed to translate content, generate ideas, and then decide how to convey those ideas in English. A common strategy I see teachers use to address the time issue is to modify the amount or type of work that multilingual students complete. They might tell students to just stop with whatever they have completed because the class must move on. This strategy can be beneficial, but it can also be discouraging. Imagine never fully completing an assignment and always being asked to move on before you were ready. While I recognize that teachers cannot always extend learning and work time until all students have completed the task, I recommend planning for adjusted time to fully complete important learning experiences and tasks when possible. It's particularly important for multilingual students to have the opportunity to complete culminating projects and be able to share completed work, so I recommend prioritizing extended time on these types of learning experiences.

Steps for instruction

1. Prior to a unit, examine essential learning experiences.
2. Identify learning experiences that could be modified or cut short that would minimally impact learning for multilingual students.
3. Identify key learning experiences for which you should prioritize full completion.
4. Plan ahead for modified instruction and extended time. This will include alternative learning experiences for students who complete learning experiences early and those who need additional time.

STRATEGY 4 Adjusted Time and Speech with Vocabulary

The National Literacy Panel on Language-Minority Children and Youth found that children learning English required more instruction in oral language development in English than their monolingual peers in order to be successful in literacy (August and Shanahan 2006). One aspect of this instruction that has been lacking is support in vocabulary knowledge and development. To better support multilingual students, teachers must constantly discuss word meanings and purposefully integrate vocabulary and oral language skills in every lesson.

Realistically, this means adjusted time for instruction and adjusted speech to better support oral language development. These adjustments are not just for tier three vocabulary or vocabulary that teachers might traditionally select to highlight for a lesson or read-aloud. This also includes "simple" vocabulary, such as the word *run*. This word has multiple meanings: someone could run for office, run down the street, run a computer program, and so on. Teachers can adjust their daily speech to include brief descriptions, examples, or rephrasing of vocabulary to help support oral language.

The following steps provide an outline for how to adjust time and speech to support vocabulary in two ways during a read-aloud: directly and indirectly. The direct version for effective vocabulary instruction is addressed in Chapter 3 and includes introducing the vocabulary with a definition or description and an example, asking students to rephrase the definition and construct a picture, symbol, or representation, and then asking students to engage in activities to add to their knowledge of a word. This is an important aspect of instruction and is often connected with teacher read-alouds. For multilingual students, I recommend also including indirect vocabulary support, where a teacher provides on-the-spot additional vocabulary reinforcement such as adding a brief description or synonym of a challenging word that they are not directly teaching.

Steps for instruction

1. Select a text for the read-aloud.
2. Plan adjusted time for slowed speech, vocabulary instruction, and additional vocabulary elaboration and conversations.
3. Identify the target academic vocabulary and plan for direct teaching.
4. Identify additional vocabulary that could be quickly supported through an aside with a synonym or brief oral definition.
5. Prepare time for students to discuss and use vocabulary in conversations related to the read-aloud.

STRATEGY 5 Adjusted Time of Teacher Support Versus Independent Work

I am an advocate for providing students extended amounts of independent time to practice and apply new learning. However, multilingual students benefit less from this independence than their monolingual peers because they need instructional support and exposure to vocabulary, syntax, and language comprehension (Escamilla et al. 2014). Yes, multilingual students still need independent time to practice, but that time is significantly more productive if the teacher provides additional and direct support to help them access grade-level content. In previous strategies, I have primarily talked about whole-class strategies, but this strategy adjusts the typical amount of independent time to include additional teacher support in small-group settings before or after whole-class instruction.

Steps for linguistic front-loading before whole-class instruction

Front-loading is particularly helpful for students in the beginning stages of language proficiency, for lessons that would not include direct vocabulary instruction, and for lessons that have text and content that are significantly beyond students' comprehension levels. This might take place once at the beginning of the week to help set students up for success.

1. Identify key concepts and vocabulary that will be addressed in the reading and writing content.
2. Find or create a modified text.
    a. Many websites and curricula have multiple versions of a text to provide differentiation. Select the level that is most appropriate.
    b. You can also use AI, such as a chatbot, to generate a text. You provide the original text and then provide prompts to adjust the length, vocabulary level, and so on.
3. Gather the small group and provide a preview of the vocabulary with a definition and visual support.
4. Highlight and have students discuss the vocabulary in their own words as they encounter it in the text.
5. Allow time for student questions and discussion.
6. Informally assess students' comprehension.
7. Provide support and prompting when necessary to build background and confidence for students to participate in the upcoming grade-level content.

Steps for small-group reinforcement after whole-class instruction

Reinforcement is particularly helpful for students who are in the middle levels of language proficiency and can access grade-level content with minimal to moderate amounts of teacher support.

1. After whole-class instruction, bring students who you anticipate need additional support together in a group.
2. Provide one to two additional opportunities for practice and application of the content introduced in the lesson.
3. Provide reinforcement and support as needed.
4. Ask students if they have questions or need additional support before moving to independent practice.
5. Support as needed.

Strategies in Action: Primary-Grade Phonemic Awareness Instruction with Adjusted Time and Speech

Sean, a kindergarten teacher, had recently been trained on a new phonological awareness and phonics curriculum that all teachers in the district were supposed to be using. He learned a great deal about providing explicit and systematic instruction for foundational skills, but some of the components were conflicting with what he thought was best for his multilingual students.

The oral drills were of particular concern. One phoneme-segmenting oral drill included the teacher saying a word quickly, asking the students how many sounds were in the word, and then having the students put their fingers up to show the number of sounds in the word. This was supposed to be repeated quickly in succession until all the words were complete. He was concerned about the speed, the lack of supports for this instruction, and more importantly a missed opportunity to support vocabulary learning and let students hear words in context to support syntax development.

The curriculum described something similar to the following for the oral drill:

1. Teacher says: "Listen to the word I say: *stem*. How many sounds are in *stem*? Count the phonemes on your fingers and use your fingers to show me how many sounds you hear."
2. Students put up fingers.
3. Teacher says: "Say the sounds."
4. Students say the sounds.

He decided to adjust time and speech to support vocabulary during his phonemic awareness instruction. He added an initial modeling exercise with student practice, visual resources, images, and a sentence to help support them. He gave all students visual manipulatives to help with the segmenting and displayed the following slide on the board.

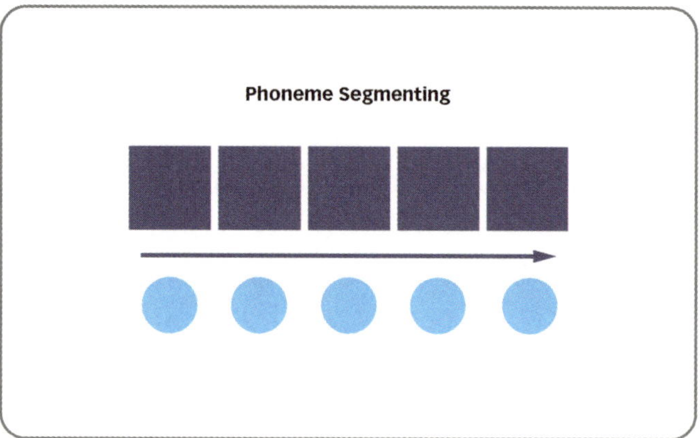

He showed the next slide and said, "We are going to listen for the sounds in a word and put a chip in a box for each sound. The word is *stem*. A flower has a stem." He pointed to the image of a flower. "The first sound I hear is /s/." He moved to the next presentation slide to show a chip moved up to the first box while saying the sound.

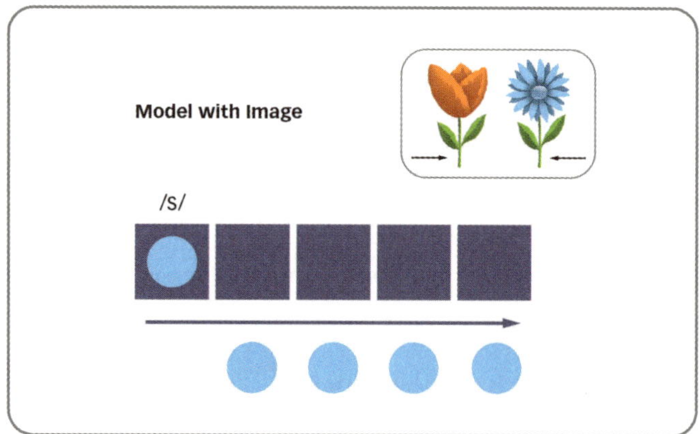

He continued, "The next sound I hear is /t/," and moved to the next slide to show a chip moved up to the second box while saying the sound.

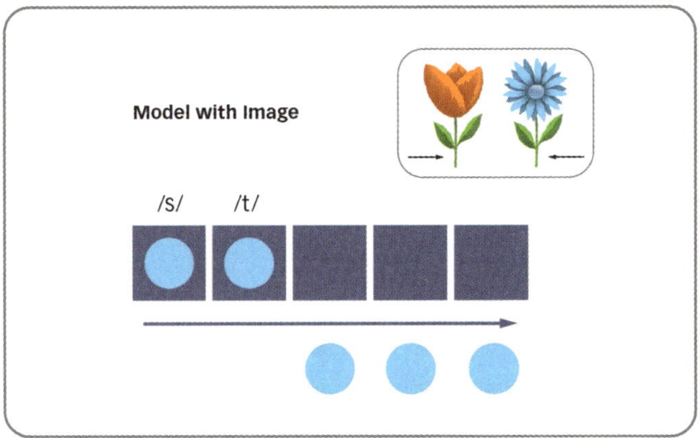

Then he said, "The next sound I hear is /ĕ/," and moved to the next slide to show a chip moved up to the third box while saying the sound.

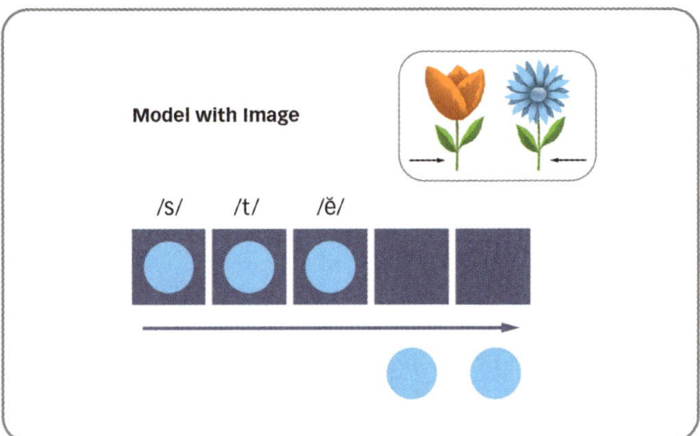

He continued, "The last sound I hear is /m/," while moving to the next slide to show another chip moved up.

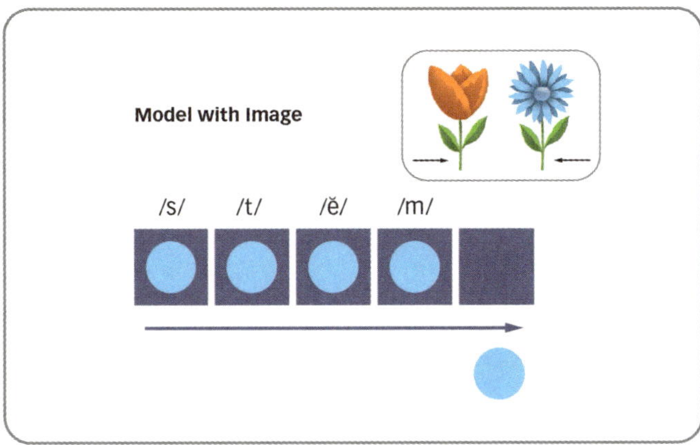

He then slid his finger across the arrow while blending the sounds to make the word *stem*. He repeated the segmenting by touching each chip while pronouncing the sound quickly, then said the entire word again while sliding across the arrow. He asked the students to do it with him using a choral response. For the last step, he asked the students to use the word in a sentence. He told them it could be the sentence he used in the introduction or they could come up with their own. They all did it successfully.

Then students were ready to try it with less support. He displayed the slide below and asked the students to use their own boxes and chips to try the new word. He said, "We are going to listen for the sounds in a word and put a chip in a box for each sound. The word is *steam*." He pointed to the image and added, "Steam is coming out of this pot. Whisper to yourself as you move a chip into a box for each sound you hear in the word *steam*."

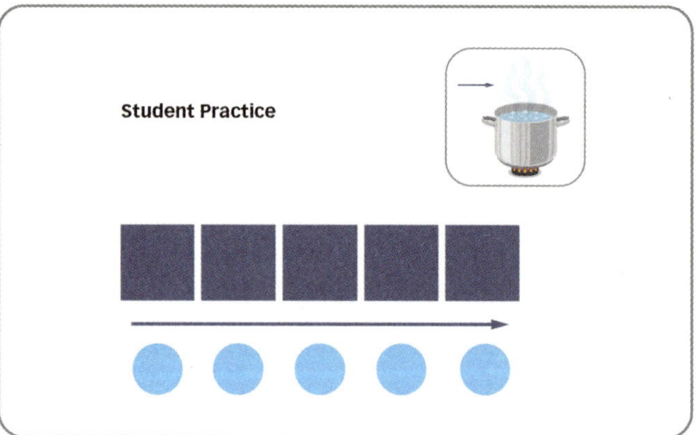

He paused and gave students a chance to practice and move their chips. Then he said, "Let's try it together. Touch a chip and say each sound, and then slide your finger on the arrow to say the entire word."

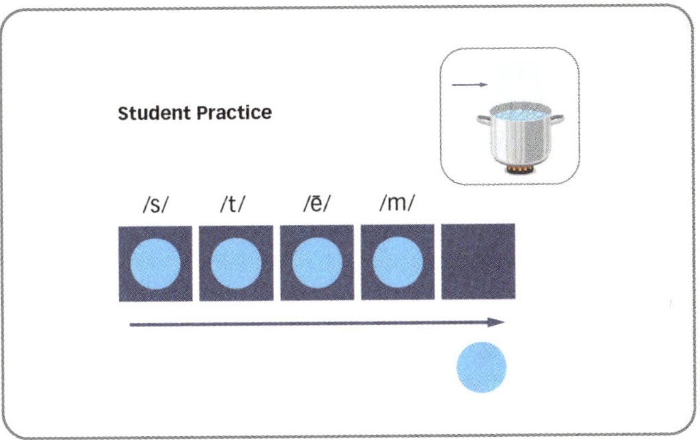

Students responded chorally while he used the board to indicate each sound. He then asked students to turn to a partner and use the word in a sentence.

Sean used a version of this strategy for all his phonological awareness and phonics activities in order to simultaneously support word recognition and vocabulary development. It did add an additional two to four minutes to the instruction, but it was worth it for him because it meant additional exposure to language for his students.

REFLECTION QUESTIONS

1. In what ways have you previously adjusted your speech to support multilingual students?
2. What challenges have you experienced with time constraints when supporting multilingual students?
3. How might you apply one or more of these strategies in your upcoming lesson or unit to support multilingual students?
4. How could you modify one of these strategies to better meet the linguistic needs of your current students' language proficiency levels?
5. How might using one or more of these strategies help students in your context?

Provide Repeated Exposure and Opportunities for Practice

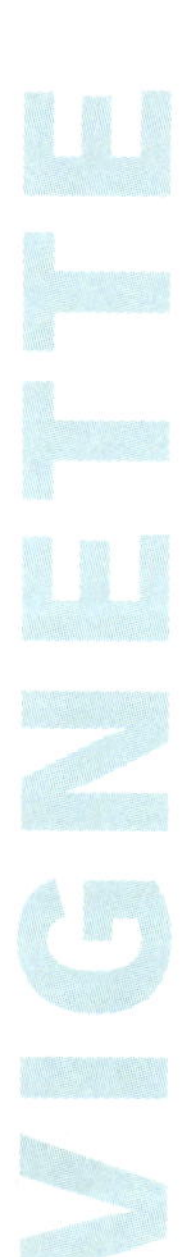

I was in a planning session with a group of fifth-grade teachers in an urban school district in which the children in their grade level spoke seven different first languages. Teachers were discussing successes and challenges of the first quarter as a way to identify pedagogical goals they wanted to address as a team for the upcoming quarter.

> **Ms. Martinez:** *I feel like the students are really working hard, and the strategies we have been using to scaffold academic vocabulary and provide access to grade-level content have been helping. During the instruction and prompted practice, students are demonstrating their new learning, but I find that after a week or so they have completely forgotten what we learned. I would like to find a way to better support retention of vocabulary and concepts.*
>
> **Mr. Jones:** *I agree. They do so well on the informal assessments, but when we revisit concepts or strategies, many of them can't recall.*

Ms. Salinas: *Same. I am also finding that because I feel like I am always short on time, they don't have enough time to really practice and internalize things. They understand what I am saying or if they read it, but they are having difficulty making it their own and using it without prompting from me.*

Me: *Some of the research is showing that it takes a minimum of ten exposures in listening, speaking, and reading to retain a new word. I find this is true with strategies or skills as well, and it often takes even more times with multilingual students because they likely won't be hearing it elsewhere. If you were estimating how many exposures students are getting, do you think it is enough?*

Teachers shook their heads no.

Ms. Salinas: *Where would I even get the time to expose them ten times?*

I agreed. Time is always a primary obstacle, but I suggested that additional repetition might be worth it if the students retained their learning. Together we brainstormed ways we could maximize time to squeeze in extra exposures without taking a ton of instructional time and how we could maintain exposures and usage after the focal instruction. The teachers came up with some great ideas: chants or mnemonic devices to reinforce simple concepts that needed to be memorized that students could say during transition times; opportunities for reinforcement games that students could play after they completed their independent learning tasks; ideas for moving beyond just the introduction of vocabulary before learning and assessing as well as including informal use and documentation. You'll see these strategies and more throughout the chapter.

The teachers set a goal of implementing one new strategy each week for increasing exposure and repetition and opportunities for practice. One teacher took the lead for the instructional strategy each week to lighten the planning load. They decided to track three to five words or concepts that were essential to literacy instruction learning each week to ensure they got a minimum of ten exposures.

When we met again at the end of the semester, I asked them how it went and had them share some successes and challenges. Here is what they said:

> **Ms. Salinas:** *In order to make it feasible with time constraints, I found that students had to be doing more of the work. It couldn't be me just providing ten exposures; they needed to use the word or strategy and practice it on multiple occasions. My favorite instructional strategies were the ones where students had to take responsibility for their repeated exposure and use.*
>
> **Ms. Martinez:** *I agree! I tried to include more exposure, but having students take accountability for using words in their discussions and track usage over the week was really powerful.*

The teachers found the focus on repeated exposure and opportunities to be helpful for retention of vocabulary, strategies, and skills. They also recognized that shifting the responsibility to students was a powerful way to give students ownership of practice and retention.

What Does the Research Say?

There is a consensus among language scholars that students need repeated exposure and opportunities to practice when learning a new language (August, Fenner, and Snyder 2014; Echevarria, Vogt, and Short 2007; Goldenberg 2013). While this seems like common sense, there can be confusion over how many exposures or how much practice learners need. Beck, McKeown, and Kucan (2013) recommend systematic instruction for vocabulary and providing a minimum of ten exposures in listening, speaking, and reading for each vocabulary word. This is likely well above the average number of exposures students have to new vocabulary.

Another challenge with repeated exposure is that it is not something that we often measure or calculate in our lesson planning beyond the focal lesson or week. Retention of vocabulary and concepts requires repetition in initial learning but also revisiting over time and across the literacy domains (reading, writing, speaking, and listening). Practice and application help in the mastering of vocabulary and skills (Fisher and Frey 2008; Marzano, Pickering, and Pollock 2001), so it is essential that we begin planning for the repeated practice and application if we want to support multilingual students' language and literacy development. This does not mean rote memorization drills and flash cards. There are many ways to provide meaningful practice and application in context. The strategies in this chapter provide research-aligned ideas for doing just that.

Five Instructional Strategies

Many of the instructional strategies in this chapter can be reused independently with students. For example, the teacher might initially provide instruction about a song or how to play a reinforcement game, but then students can use it independently during the unit and also beyond to continue to revisit and reinforce vocabulary, strategies, and skills.

STRATEGY 1 Songs and Chants

There is some content that is beneficial to memorize. It takes multiple exposures and repetition to do this. One fun and easy way to do this is with songs or chants. These can be repeated during transition times such as lining up for recess or lunch or on students' way to the carpet.

The most common songs you might remember include songs to learn your ABCs (there are songs with just the letters and other songs that include sounds or words that correspond with the letters), body parts ("Head, Shoulders, Knees, and Toes"), cleanup songs, counting songs, math concept songs, songs about grammar, and so on.

Chants are also common instructional tools. Skip-counting chants or chants about how many days are in each month are common practice in early literacy contexts. All help provide additional exposure to the concept and language related to the instruction. For multilingual students, I add some additional components for the first couple of times they are exposed to the song or chant.

Steps for instruction

1. You can do an internet search or use AI, such as a chatbot, to search for most basic concepts and vocabulary you want to teach in a song.
2. Instead of just singing the song and using oral language, also provide a written text to accompany the chant or song.
3. Add some type of visuals with the written text.
4. Try to add physical movement or gestures with the concept.

FIGURE 7.1 *Threw or Through?*

I also sometimes make up my own songs. I have an entire series for homophones to help my multilingual students remember them. Making your own songs is simpler than you might think. First, identify content you want to teach. Then select a familiar tune or song and write words that teach the content to the beat of the song. The example in Figure 7.1 shows how I teach the spelling of the homophone *through*. This includes the physical movement of going through a bridge, is set to the familiar song "London Bridge Is Falling Down," and emphasizes the tricky part of spelling the word.

STRATEGY 2 Reinforcement Games

The list of reinforcement games is extensive: bingo, picture-matching memory, Mad Libs®, Jeopardy!®, Trivial Pursuit®, crossword puzzles, charades, Who am I? (a game where students have to ask questions to guess the word or name they have taped on their back), Heads Up! (discussed in Chapter 3), and so on. The key to making these effective is first selecting words and concepts that are essential to learning in the unit. I typically use the vocabulary words from my current instruction during the first round of play to reinforce current learning. Once students have played it with my direction and support, it then becomes one of the things students can do when they have completed their independent learning tasks, during choice time, or during inside recess.

However, reinforcement games are also great for revisiting previously learned vocabulary and content. I also create another game that includes content from two to three units, so the memory game or trivia game will challenge students to revisit previously learned vocabulary and content. There are many free online resources for generating your own bingo games, trivia games, crossword puzzles, and other games.

Steps for instruction

1. Identify key vocabulary, questions, or concepts for the game.
2. Use a game generator to input your content, or create your own game.
3. Laminate game pieces to use throughout the semester or year and for future years.
4. Introduce how to play the game after initial instruction on the focal content.
5. Support students in playing the game (establish roles and rules).
6. Place in a games area or area where students have resources for independent work or things to do when they are done with independent work.
7. Encourage students to continue playing.

For example, here are two versions of bingo for the same content with different levels of difficulty. One person reads the definition on a card aloud, and the other players look for the word that matches that definition on their bingo boards. An alternative to reading the card aloud could be holding up a picture. See Figure 7.2 for the simplified bingo board (in which any three in a row win) and Figure 7.3 for a couple of sample definition cards. See Figure 7.4 for the more advanced game, in which you need five in a row to win, requiring exposure to and knowledge of more vocabulary.

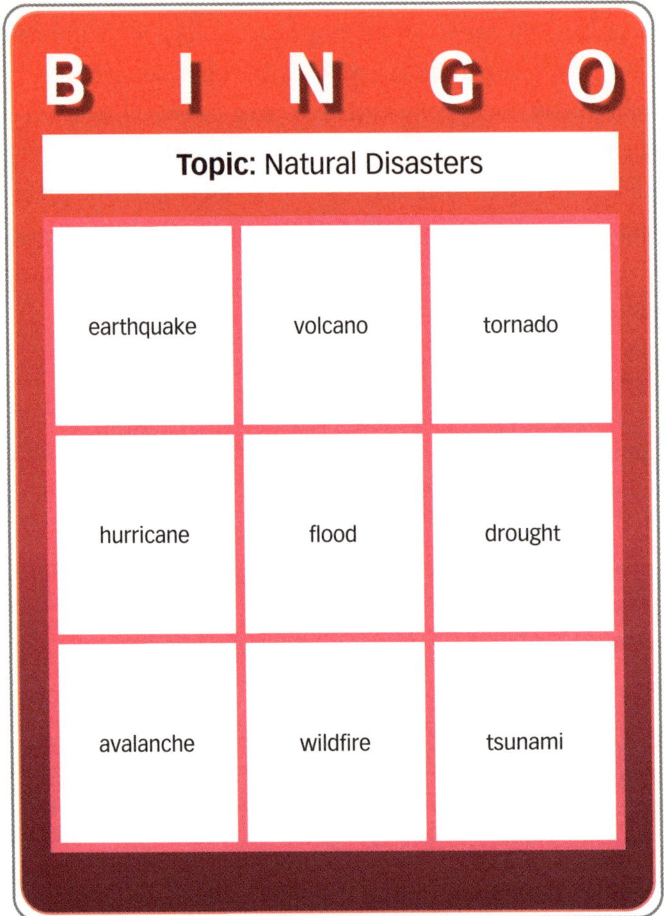

FIGURE 7.2 *Simplified Natural Disaster Bingo*

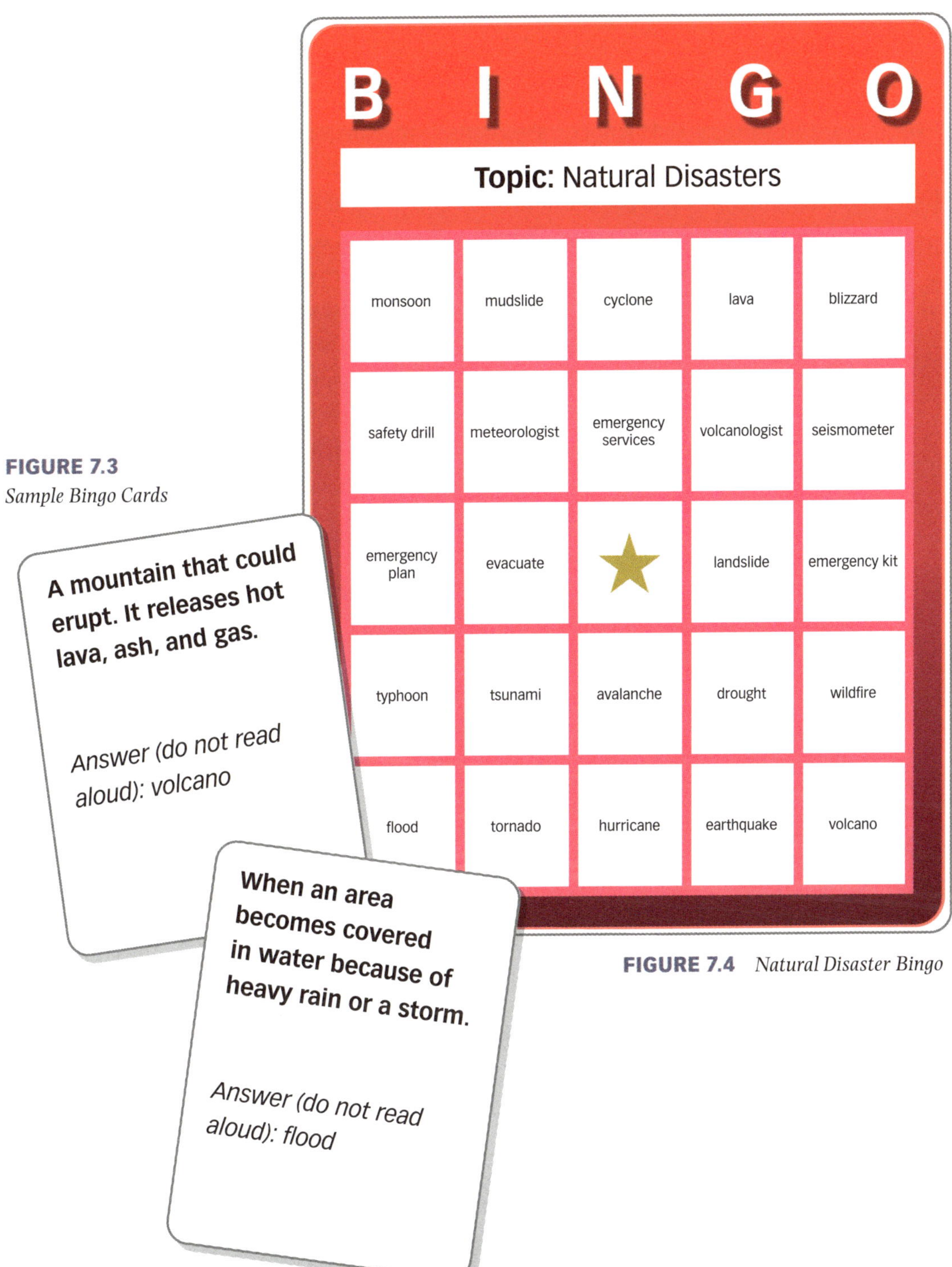

FIGURE 7.3 *Sample Bingo Cards*

FIGURE 7.4 *Natural Disaster Bingo*

STRATEGY 3 Vocabulary Tracking

Many teachers of multilingual students try to find ways to encourage student use of new vocabulary. I have seen vocabulary word chains, where teachers add a link to a paper chain when students use new vocabulary without prompting. Then, when the chain is long enough to reach across the room, they have a word detective party. Other teachers just encourage students to try to use new vocabulary in their writing and conversations. All of these are beginning strategies for helping students be more metacognitive about their vocabulary usage.

I have found giving students ownership and responsibility related to their vocabulary learning and usage is a very powerful way to provide multiple exposures and opportunities for practice. I created a vocabulary-tracking organizer to help students document pre-, during-, and postinstruction vocabulary usage. It starts with a focus on the teacher-introduced vocabulary that often takes place before instruction. Then, during the instruction, students can use tally marks to document the teachers' usage of the vocabulary. After instruction, the teacher gives two partner talk opportunities. During the partner talk, students tally the number of times their partner uses a vocabulary word. I find that having a concrete focus and tracker increases students' awareness and this leads to increased exposures and usage of the new target vocabulary. I do not do this with every lesson I teach, but it is a great strategy for the start to a new unit or series of lessons where there will be important new vocabulary students will need to be successful.

I often leave the organizer as you see it in Figure 7.5 (see also OR 7–1 in the Online Resources) and ask the students to fill it out. However, for more support, the teacher could fill in the topic, teacher-introduced vocabulary, and partner talk instructions.

Steps for instruction

1. Identify key vocabulary that will be essential for learning and participating in an introductory lesson. The vocabulary should be

OR 7–1

VOCABULARY TRACKER

Name: ______________________________

Topic: ______________________________

Teacher-Introduced Vocabulary	Tally Marks for Times Used During Instruction

Partner Talk Instructions or Prompts:

1. ______________________________

2. ______________________________

› Prepare your thinking or response with notes in the boxes below.
› Share your response with supporting evidence and using teacher-introduced vocabulary.
› Listen to your partner and add a tally for each time your partner uses a vocabulary word.

Response Notes for Prompt 1	Response Notes for Prompt 2

Response Prompt 1		Response Prompt 2	
Vocabulary Words Used	Tally Marks	Vocabulary Words Used	Tally Marks

FIGURE 7.5 *Vocabulary Tracker* OR 7–1

words that students will see on more than a single occasion.

2. Identify two open-ended partner discussion prompts that would provide opportunities for students to reflect on learning and use the newly introduced vocabulary.
3. Create a graphic organizer for tracking vocabulary or use the one in the Online Resources (OR 7–1). Depending on student needs,

you can fill in the teacher-introduced vocabulary list and the partner talk instructions or prompts.

4. Give each student a copy of the vocabulary tracker and explain how to use it and the benefit of thinking about vocabulary and expanding usage of new vocabulary.
5. Clearly introduce the new vocabulary prior to instruction.
6. Plan to use the vocabulary throughout the reading or instruction.
7. Provide students with the two partner talk prompts or instructions for discussion.
8. Give students a couple of minutes to think and write down notes to prepare for partner talk.
9. Ask students to take turns discussing their thinking. Remind them to tally their partner's vocabulary usage.
10. Ask the class to reflect on the content and discussion. Ask the class to reflect on their vocabulary usage. Encourage them to find ways to use this vocabulary over the next series of lessons.

STRATEGY 4 Goal Setting and Monitoring

We often introduce a concept, skill, or goal for students that receives our attention and their attention for a couple of days or a week. Then, we move on to something new and the focus on those previously taught concepts slowly fades away. However, there are certain goals that span longer periods of time and multiple instructional areas. These goals deserve continued monitoring by the teacher and the students. This monitoring and reflection is also a great way to continue to draw attention to important concepts and skills.

Hopefully, teachers set goals in coordination with students and differentiate them according to their strengths and needs. I recommend conscientiously planning opportunities for you and your students to assess their goal progress on multiple learning experiences throughout the semester. The examples you see here show a range of rubrics for self-checking and teacher checking of student writing. Tam, a second-grade teacher in Australia, has seven different versions, all with different levels of complexity, some of which are shown in Figure 7.6 (see also OR 7–2 in the Online Resources for all seven versions). Most components of the rubric include words or are self-explanatory but a couple that might need clarification include the following: the picture of a person represents character description, the *C* represents capital letters at the start of a sentence, and the dot with a face in it represents a period. As students continually demonstrate success with their goals,

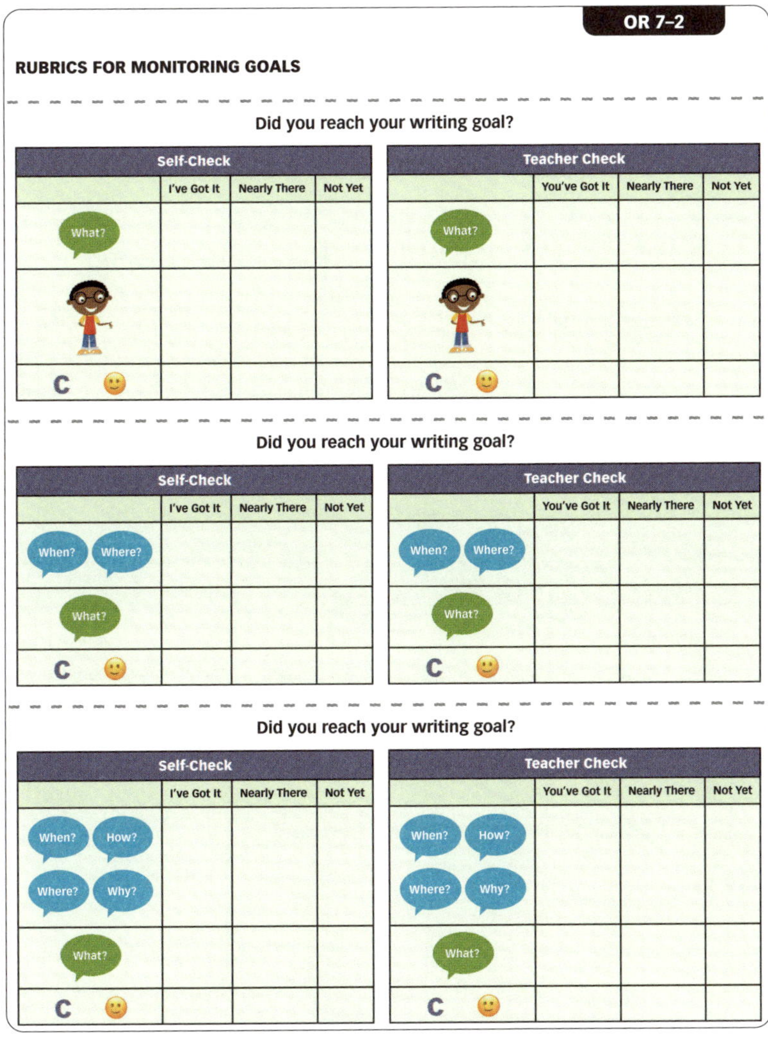

OR 7–2

RUBRICS FOR MONITORING GOALS

Did you reach your writing goal?

Self-Check			
	I've Got It	Nearly There	Not Yet
What?			
C			

Teacher Check			
	You've Got It	Nearly There	Not Yet
What?			
C			

Did you reach your writing goal?

Self-Check			
	I've Got It	Nearly There	Not Yet
When? Where?			
What?			
C			

Teacher Check			
	You've Got It	Nearly There	Not Yet
When? Where?			
What?			
C			

Did you reach your writing goal?

Self-Check			
	I've Got It	Nearly There	Not Yet
When? How? Where? Why?			
What?			
C			

Teacher Check			
	You've Got It	Nearly There	Not Yet
When? How? Where? Why?			
What?			
C			

FIGURE 7.6 *Rubrics for Monitoring Goals* OR 7–2

they reset the goals to be more challenging, and she adjusts the rubric they use. She has copies of these cut out and can add them to students' reading or writing notebooks for periodic goal-setting checks with formal and informal reading responses.

In Figure 7.7, you can see the student added a self-check to a draft of writing in her writing notebook. Tam reads the notebooks at the end of the week and adds the teacher check and provides feedback to their writing. The evolving monitoring helps provide students with repeated exposure to learning goals, regardless of the specific lesson focus.

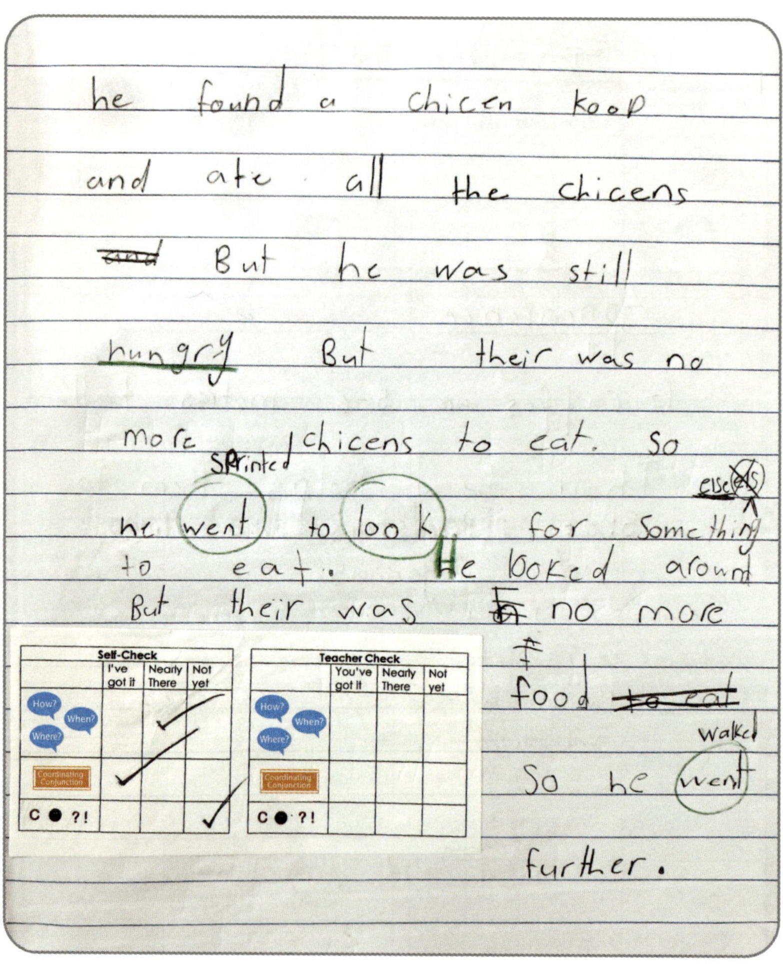

FIGURE 7.7 *Sample of Student Self-Check*

Steps for instruction

1. Identify broad grade-level or language-proficiency goals that students would use across multiple lessons and extended time periods. Typically, the majority of this content is content you have previously taught or will be teaching within the semester.
2. Create a range of sophistication for self-check and teacher-check rubrics that is appropriate for your context, grade level, and language proficiency levels. The example had an extensive range, but three levels would be a good place to start. You can begin to refine and extend from there.
3. Use an initial student sample (writing response, reading response, etc.) to confer with the student to identify strengths and goals they are already consistently meeting.
4. With the student, select from the range of goals what they think would be an attainable goal to consistently demonstrate in their work.
5. Give them a copy of the rubric to put in their notebook for reference.
6. Tell them that they can use it to help them remember and self-check at any time and that you will also do periodic check-ins.
7. Identify upcoming learning experiences where goal monitoring would be helpful and appropriate.
8. Give students rubrics to glue into their responses for self-reflection.
9. Complete teacher reflection and provide feedback.
10. Adjust goals as necessary.

STRATEGY 5 Connected and Integrated Units

One helpful strategy for maximizing exposure and usage of vocabulary and newly learned concepts is to connect them across content areas and purposefully embed exposure and repetition wherever possible. This instructional strategy greatly depends on how much curricular freedom teachers have in their context. Schools that use an inquiry-based approach to teaching and learning have this repetition built in to instruction as students explore the focal topic of inquiry in reading, writing, math, science, and social studies. For other contexts, connected and integrated reading and writing units are the most feasible option.

It is logical and efficient to have reading instruction support writing instruction and vice versa. Academic vocabulary and literary concepts (character traits, plot development, genre, text features, voice, etc.) that you're introducing in reading can help provide ideas and examples for strategies students might use as writers. I typically begin the instruction with reading. We notice and name the target concepts, analyze text to find examples of the concept, and discuss the purpose the author might have had in developing the concept in this way. Then, in writing, we draw on the learning and analysis in reading to inspire use of these concepts and writing techniques. This repetition helps students see and hear vocabulary and concepts across instructional areas to solidify their understanding.

Steps for instruction

1. Prior to the start of the year, look across your units or areas of focus to try to find overlap or units that you could connect.
2. Plan to teach these units simultaneously or close in time span.
3. Identify vocabulary and concepts that you can connect and reinforce.
4. Plan for the introduction and opportunities for practice and use of essential connected vocabulary and concepts.
5. If needed, create an anchor chart or planning graphic organizer to help support students. In the example in Figure 7.8 (see also OR 7–3 in the Online Resources), the chart names the element that was introduced in reading with an example from a published book and the author's purpose. Then, it has space for students to document how they might use it in their own writing.

Narrative Stories			
Element	**Example from Story**	**Author's Purpose**	**Ideas for My Writing**
Setting description			
Interesting introduction			
Character development			
Plot with problem			
Solution			

FIGURE 7.8 *Narrative Stories* OR 7–3

Strategies in Action: Primary-Grade Play

Paula Garces, a kindergarten teacher in Medellín, Colombia, and I worked together on a language and literacy research project. All of the students in her classroom were newly learning English. For the research project, Paula set a goal of increasing students' independent use of social vocabulary that might be used at a restaurant. Together we developed an intervention based on literacy and play and studied its effectiveness. This is an example of a connected and integrated unit amplified.

We started by reading a book aloud to students, introducing vocabulary and sentence stems to scaffold interactions. Then we had students practice in pairs, gave them printed menus with photos, and modeled language and play in a restaurant in the play area.

However, one of the things we learned quickly was that students needed and benefited from extensive exposure and opportunities to practice using new vocabulary. We also found that both structured opportunities with support from a teacher and independent opportunities benefited learning and retention of new language. In order to support this learning and meet the academic needs, we designed a book with visual supports, color-coding, controlled vocabulary, and clear sentence stems (underlined) that would model language students could use in the play center. We used this book as a read-aloud but then also for small-group guided reading with students. See the sample pages in Figures 7.9, 7.10, and 7.11.

Then we added a new small-group rotation of supported play and reading. Here we introduced new sentence stems, menus, and vocabulary along with

FIGURE 7.9 *Book Page 1*

FIGURE 7.10 *Book Page 2*

FIGURE 7.11 *Book Page 5*

FIGURE 7.12 *Supported Play Group*

play materials. Students took turns reading sentence stems and playing with a partner as a teacher supported with language, as shown in Figure 7.12.

We also included a small-group rotation that started as word work using letter tiles to spell words they would use in a restaurant (seen Figure 7.13). This evolved into a writing center where students used sentence stems and picture cards to write and illustrate about restaurant concepts (see Figure 7.14).

FIGURE 7.13 *Letter Tiles Station*

FIGURE 7.14 *Writing Center*

With all the repetition, continued exposure to new vocabulary, and opportunities for supported and independent practice, we saw a significant increase in independent English usage. Students felt confident and successful using the language because they had been seeing it, hearing it, saying it, and writing it in every aspect of literacy time.

REFLECTION QUESTIONS

1. How are you currently providing opportunities for repeated exposure and practice?
2. Do you feel your multilingual students are getting enough exposure and practice to retain vocabulary and concepts?
3. What are some challenges you have experienced with providing repeated exposure and opportunities for practice?
4. How might you implement one of these strategies to better support your multilingual students in an upcoming lesson or unit?
5. What modifications could you make to these strategies to better fit the needs of your multilingual students?

Prepare Resources to Support Student Responses

VIGNETTE

David recently started teaching fifth grade after ten years as a primary-grade teacher. While all of his teaching career included work with multilingual students learning English at varying stages of proficiency, he found the new level of content and language complexity daunting. He said, "Teaching is never easy, but it was so much easier to support academic vocabulary and content for my beginning speakers when it was at a first-grade level. The grade-level language and content are so complex that it feels really difficult to scaffold enough for my more beginning speakers."

David was particularly challenged as the class began an integrated science and literacy unit on climate change. In the previous integrated unit, just introducing vocabulary at the start of the lesson was not enough to give his beginning speakers access to the science content or communicate their understanding of the complex material. For this unit, he strategically planned to front-load and reinforce vocabulary and content before, during, and after reading and provided modified text for independent research work. He used visuals and definitions and drew attention to vocabulary throughout instruction, but he also started creating guided or cloze notes for each lesson.

You will read more about these in the strategy section, but they were notes that covered the key vocabulary and content of the lesson and reading. However, instead of just summarizing the content for students, David strategically omitted key words and vocabulary to make the notes interactive, like you would see in a cloze activity. This allowed students to contribute to the note-taking and focus on key vocabulary and content without being overwhelmed by language. David then asked students to draw on these notes to participate in conversations with their research groups. David said these prepared resources for accessing content and having conversations with peers made a significant difference in the participation of his beginning speakers.

What Does the Research Say?

Multilingual students benefit from multiple opportunities to practice and respond to new learning. However, not all responses and preparation to respond are equal. Open-ended questions or prompts can feel overwhelming to students newly learning a language. Providing prepared supports such as word banks, sentence stems, graphic organizers, summary frames, and cloze or guided notes can scaffold using new vocabulary and responding in complete sentences (Echevarria, Vogt, and Short 2007). These frames can provide a language model and assist multilingual learners in practicing subject-verb agreement. Most importantly, these instructional strategies can help multilingual students participate more fully with decreased anxiety about language production. For beginning speakers, these strategies can be simple and straightforward. As students gain language proficiency, they benefit from having less scaffolding. Teachers can easily adjust sentence stems to more complex sentences with possibilities for open-ended responses for students who are ready for it.

Note-taking is an essential skill that can feel overwhelming for multilingual students, but taking notes improves student learning (Kiewra 2002; Chang and Ku 2015). An effective scaffold for students not yet ready to independently take extensive notes is providing guided notes (a strategy discussed in more depth later in the chapter). The use of teacher-created guided notes with an outline and support material appropriate to student needs with space for students to complete key information has been documented to increase student achievement across all ages (Haydon et al. 2011).

Five Instructional Strategies

The key with all these instructional strategies is preparing resources ahead of time so that multilingual students can successfully document what they are learning. Then they can use this scaffolded documentation to participate in discussions, assignments, and larger projects. A focus on language complexity and opportunities for student output (writing and speaking) when preparing these resources will set the students up for success and build confidence. The following instructional strategies and classroom examples build from this research.

STRATEGY 1 Word Banks

Word banks are probably the simplest and most straightforward instructional strategy for preparing resources to support student responses. These can take on a range of forms. Some of the most basic word banks might include a visual with a corresponding word. A common version of this for very beginning speakers is for communicating their emotions or feelings. The word bank would include a possible response to how they are feeling with a corresponding picture.

I have commonly seen teachers and students create word banks to use in their writing and oral language. This might include a series of synonyms or more sophisticated words to use for common vocabulary. The example in Figure 8.1 could be used when studying character traits.

Instead of *nice* . . .	**Instead of *mean* . . .**
kind	unkind
sweet	selfish
thoughtful	greedy
considerate	spiteful
polite	obnoxious
generous	malicious
friendly	disagreeable
Instead of *smart* . . .	**Instead of *bad* . . .**
intelligent	terrible
wise	horrible
savvy	awful
clever	atrocious
brilliant	corrupt
sharp	vicious

FIGURE 8.1 *Word Bank*

Another version of a word bank includes a list of words at the top of the page to complete a cloze activity summarizing a book or reading passage, like the one in Figure 8.2.

Name: ______________________________

Word Bank

laborers	tragedy	resilience	adversity
privileged	prejudice	determination	challenges

Use the words above to summarize your reading of *Esperanza Rising*:

"Esperanza Rising" is a novel written by Pam Muñoz Ryan telling the story of a young Mexican girl named Esperanza who faces significant ____________ and changes in her life. After a ____________, she and her mother must leave their ____________ life in Mexico and work as farm ____________ in California during the Great Depression. Through hard work, ____________, and the support of newfound friends, Esperanza learns to adapt to her new life, confront ______________, and find strength in herself. The novel explores themes of ______________, family, and the pursuit of the American dream amid ______________.

Cloze created from summary pulled from ChatGPT.

Answers:

"Esperanza Rising" is a novel written by Pam Muñoz Ryan, telling the story of a young Mexican girl named Esperanza who faces significant challenges and changes in her life. After a tragedy, she and her mother must leave their privileged life in Mexico and work as farm laborers in California during the Great Depression. Through hard work, determination, and the support of newfound friends, Esperanza learns to adapt to her new life, confront prejudice, and find strength in herself. The novel explores themes of resilience, family, and the pursuit of the American Dream amidst adversity.

FIGURE 8.2 *Word Bank with Cloze*

A more challenging version of a word bank on the same topic might have open-ended directions that require students to use all of the words in their response. See the example in Figure 8.3.

Name: ______________________________

Word Bank

laborers	tragedy	resilience	adversity
privileged	prejudice	determination	challenges

Use the words above to summarize your reading of *Esperanza Rising*:

____
____
____
____
____
____
____
____
____
____
____
____

FIGURE 8.3 *Challenging Word Bank*

Steps for instruction

1. Identify key vocabulary.
2. Decide on the appropriate level of scaffolding needed to support student responses.
3. Generate a word bank to accompany oral or written responses.

STRATEGY 2 Sentence Stems

Sentence stems are a helpful resource to support students in speaking in complete sentences. Teachers can model the sentence or question stems to prepare students to respond. Using sentence stems in preparation for student talk and response allows students to practice more sophisticated language structures, expanding from simple one-word answers. It also decreases the stress and anxiety around sentence structure for beginning speakers and allows them to focus on content and how they will communicate what they know.

Like word banks, sentence stems can take on a wide range of sophistication. For very beginning speakers, we might create an interactive sentence stem chart with images. One example of this might be learning about the community, as shown in Figure 8.4. The teacher could model using the interactive sentence stem chart and then encourage students to practice with partners.

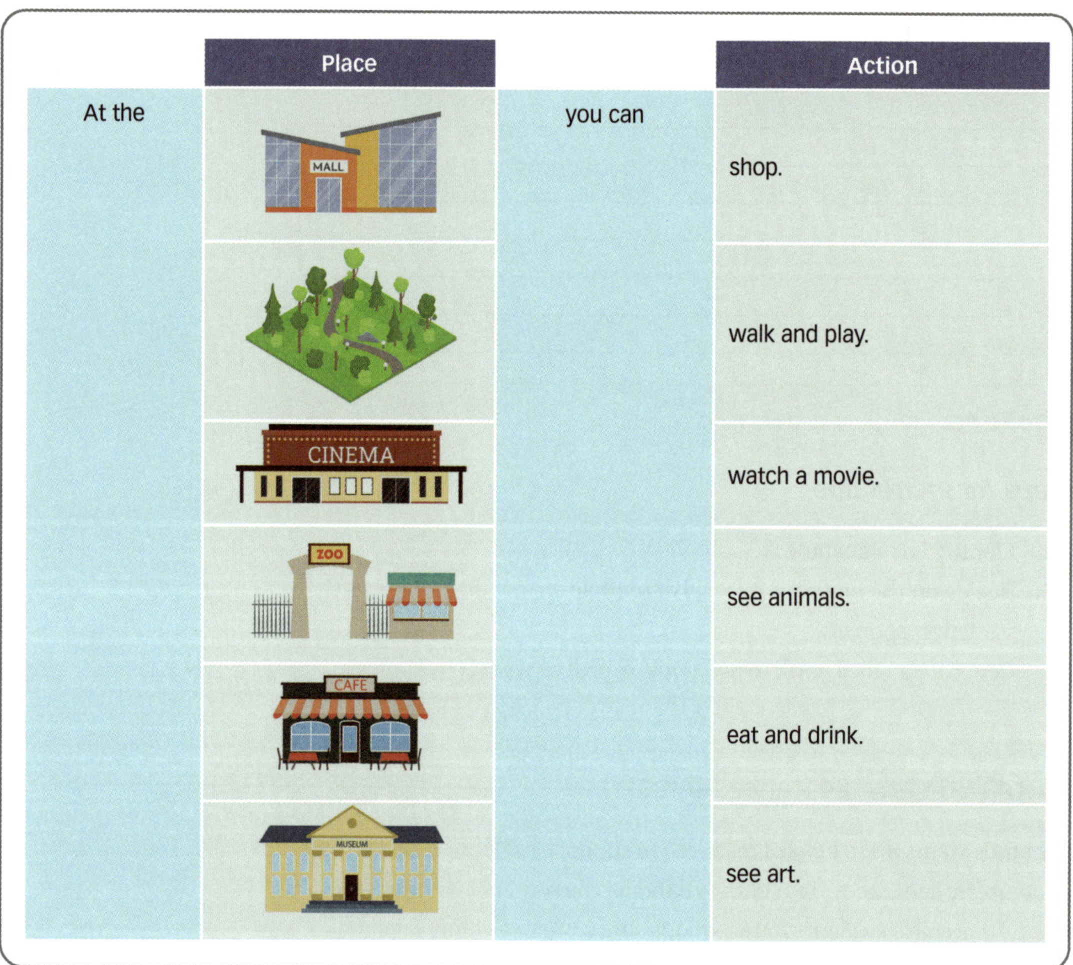

FIGURE 8.4 *Sentence Stem Chart*

Once students move beyond basic communication, teachers can create more open-ended sentence stems. As mentioned in Chapter 4, I like to provide a sentence stem to accompany literacy strategies that I teach. These are typically straightforward and might be something as simple as "This book reminds me of ______________." Or, as seen in the previous chapter in the literacy-and-play-based unit, we introduced multiple sentence stems that could facilitate ongoing interaction during play (asking what they wanted to order, ordering, asking the cost, paying the bill, etc.).

Many teachers also create a list of sentence stems to support student-led discussions. Depending on the age range and level of language proficiency, this typically includes a series of responses that will help guide and extend conversations. Figure 8.5 is a first-grade version.

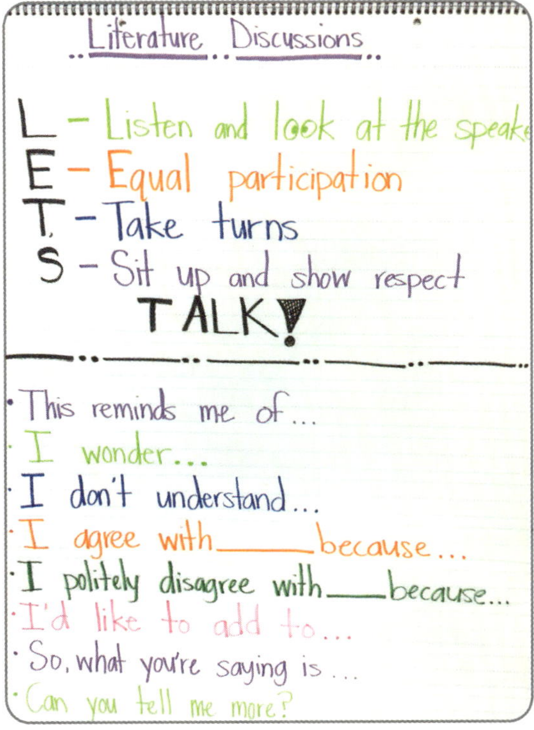

FIGURE 8.5 *Literature Discussion Sentence Stems*

Literature discussion sentence stems can easily be adjusted in complexity for older and more proficient students. Teachers can generate these stems based on the instruction they have been providing and goals related to both language and literacy, or they can do a quick search online for sentence stems, topic, and grade level to find resources created by other educators.

Steps for instruction

1. Identify opportunities for student response and discussion.
2. Generate discussion or response topics related to learning objectives.
3. Create sentence stems to support student responses.
    a. These can be basic and highly structured for beginning speakers.

b. These can be structured but open ended for students in the middle ranges of proficiency.

c. These can be extensive, varied, and selected by students from a wide range of choices for discussion for students in the middle to higher ranges of proficiency.

STRATEGY 3 Graphic Organizers

Graphic organizers are visual tools that help support multilingual students in the processing, recording, and organizing of information. They can take on many different forms, from teacher-created and highly structured to student-made and open ended. I have introduced graphic organizers such as the Frayer Model, semantic maps, and the RAN chart in earlier chapters. Graphic organizers can help students compare information, as seen in one of the most commonly used graphic organizers, the Venn diagram. Graphic organizers are also used to help students

FIGURE 8.6 *Narrative Story Planner Example*

document their understanding or summarize reading material. In Figure 8.6, you can see the teacher created a structured graphic organizer related to the class read-aloud to teach and reinforce the components of summarizing a narrative and connecting that to what writers do when planning a narrative. Students could use words, images, or both to show what they knew.

Other graphic organizers can help teach students a process, such as the scientific method or how to craft a persuasive essay. While these seem like simple instructional strategies, they can be particularly helpful for multilingual learners who are still acquiring academic vocabulary. The visual representations and breakdown of material into separate visual categories helps simplify and clarify steps that the teacher often introduces orally. It can also take an overwhelming task like writing an informational report, and break it down into accessible steps, as shown in Figure 8.7 (see also OR 8–1 in the Online Resources). Using graphic organizers as preparation for completing a long and more formalized process or writing product can also be helpful for

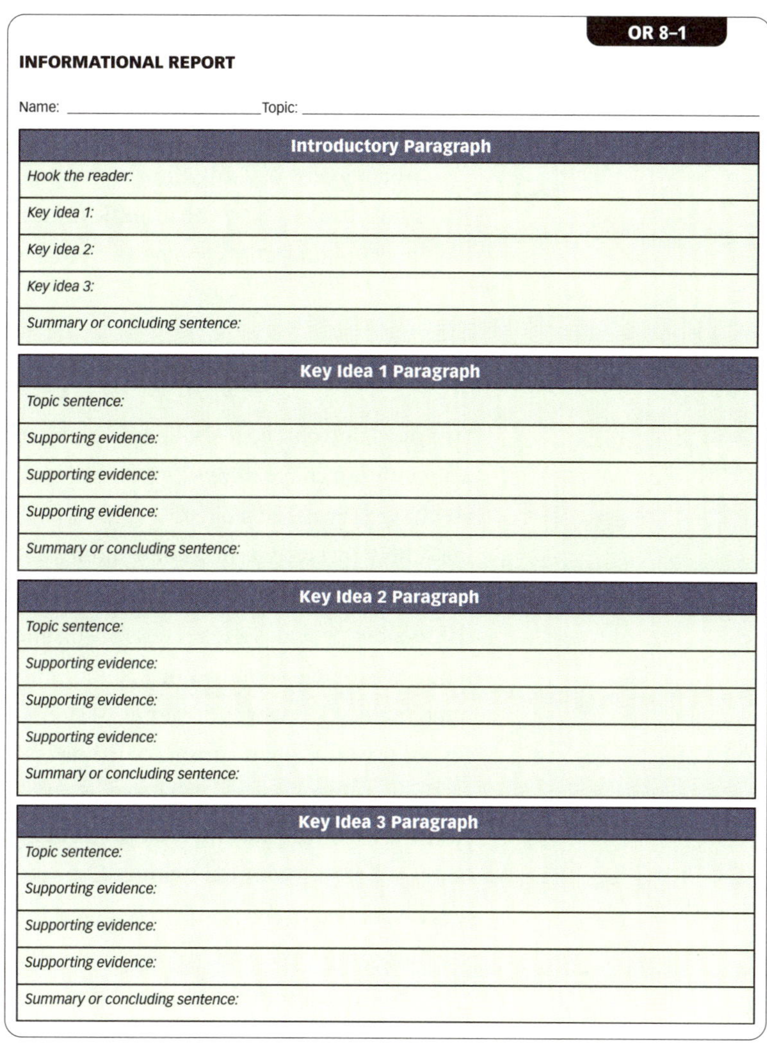

OR 8–1

INFORMATIONAL REPORT

Name: ____________________ Topic: ____________________

Introductory Paragraph
Hook the reader:
Key idea 1:
Key idea 2:
Key idea 3:
Summary or concluding sentence:

Key Idea 1 Paragraph
Topic sentence:
Supporting evidence:
Supporting evidence:
Supporting evidence:
Summary or concluding sentence:

Key Idea 2 Paragraph
Topic sentence:
Supporting evidence:
Supporting evidence:
Supporting evidence:
Summary or concluding sentence:

Key Idea 3 Paragraph
Topic sentence:
Supporting evidence:
Supporting evidence:
Supporting evidence:
Summary or concluding sentence:

FIGURE 8.7 *Informational Report Graphic Organizer* OR 8–1

informal assessment and teacher support prior to the completion and assessment of the project.

Graphic organizers are easy to find online, but they are also simple to create and adjust to meet the needs of any instructional goals.

Steps for instruction

1. Identify the goal of instruction and student response (compare and contrast, summarize a story, document a process, prepare for writing, etc.).
2. Select an appropriate graphic organizer to align with the goals of instruction (Venn diagram, table, chart, pyramid, sequence, map, etc.).
3. Model how to use the graphic organizer and discuss the purposes and benefits of using the graphic organizer.
4. Have students use the graphic organizer, and provide support and peer collaboration opportunities as needed.

STRATEGY 4 Summary Frames

Summarizing can be a challenging concept made even more difficult by academic language difficulties for students learning a new language. If you have ever asked a classful of students to write a summary, you have inevitably received a range of responses, from every detail in the story to a blank page and an overwhelmed student. With summary frames, the teacher provides the process of summarizing while also providing language to help support and sequence an academic summary. These often include keywords or sentence stems to support students. Probably the most well-known summary frame is the somebody-wanted-but-so-then strategy (Beers 2002; Serravallo 2015). This helps students summarize by prompting them to identify the main characters (somebody), what they wanted (wanted), the problem (but), how the characters responded to the problem (so), and how it all concluded (then). This is a quick and easy strategy that helps students summarize a story.

For multilingual students, I like to combine sentence stems and visual tools to provide additional support and emphasize important academic vocabulary. This is particularly critical when we're moving into more sophisticated content and I want students to use academic language and expand sentence structure in their response. Figure 8.8 is a summary frame within a graphic organizer with sentence stems (see also OR 8–2 in the Online Resources).

Summary frames can take on varying levels of content and linguistic complexity, depending on the needs of your students.

Steps for instruction

1. Identify the complexity of the desired summary (one simple sentence versus a long paragraph, for example).
2. Select academic language and grammatical structures you want to introduce or reinforce during your students' responses.
3. Design a summary frame with or without visual supports like a graphic organizer.
4. Include some type of analysis or interpretation in addition to the basic summary—ideally, a concept

OR 8–2

SUMMARY

Name:____________________

OVERVIEW

In the story ________________ by the author ________________, the main character, ________________, is ________________________________.

The conflict in the story is ________________________________.

SEQUENCE

First, ________________________________.

Next, ________________________________.

Then, to resolve the conflict, ________________________________.

Finally, ________________________________.

ANALYSIS OR INTERPRETATION

The theme of this story is ________________________________.

FIGURE 8.8 *Summary Frame* OR 8–2

such as theme, mood, or author's intention that has already been discussed in class.

5. Model for students using a shared text.
6. Ask students to use the summary frame to document their comprehension of a text they are reading independently.

STRATEGY 5 Guided and Cloze Notes

Note-taking is an important strategy that helps students document information and has been shown to improve student learning (Chang and Ku 2015; Rahmani and Sadeghi 2011). Note-taking helps with retention of information but can also be used as a starting point for peer discussion and as a resource for assignments and studying. However, taking notes from reading grade-level texts and listening to lectures can feel overwhelming for students. Some teachers prepare notes and give them to students, but research has shown that the retention of material is greater when students are active learners, not just passive receivers of content.

Two helpful options for multilingual students are guided and cloze notes. For students who need the most support, I use cloze notes. Cloze notes are essentially all of the teacher's notes with key vocabulary omitted for students to complete. Sometimes these also include a word bank at the top of the notes to support students' completion.

Steps for cloze notes

1. Complete notes for the instructional content or reading you're going to cover.
2. Remove key vocabulary and replace with blank spaces for students to fill in.
3. Create a word bank (optional) with essential vocabulary.
4. Give students a copy prior to the lesson and tell them how to complete it during the lecture or reading.
5. Tell students to use the notes as a resource during peer discussions, completion of assignments, and studying.

Guided notes are sometimes also called skeleton notes, and the teacher prepares an outline of the key material, leaving space for students to complete notes in the essential areas. I typically use these types of notes for students in the middle ranges of proficiency because they are prepared for the more open-ended structure. For additional support and retention, I also add a column for a visual representation. See the example in Figure 8.9.

Steps for guided notes

1. Identify three to five key areas students would need to document during note-taking.
2. Create a chart with key elements, space for students to take notes, and an area for a visual sketch.
3. Model and explain how to use the guided notes.
4. Ask students to complete the notes during the lecture or reading.
5. Have students work with partners to review and revise their notes.
6. Encourage students to use the notes as a resource during discussions, completion of assignments, and studying.

Cesar Chavez		
	Notes	**Sketch**
Childhood		
Political Beliefs		
Significant Achievements		

FIGURE 8.9 *Guided Notes*

Strategies in Action: Primary-Grade Resources to Support Student Response

Tam, a second-grade teacher, often uses graphic organizers to support her students. For a narrative writing unit, she decided to strategically connect reading and writing instruction. During reading, she had students use a graphic organizer, as discussed in Strategy 3, to document the key components of the story they read. She asked students to reflect on how they thought the author would have planned for creating this story. The graphic organizer helped all students, regardless of their proficiency level, to document the characters, setting, beginning, middle, and end of the story. It also prepared them to use it as a tool to plan their own stories.

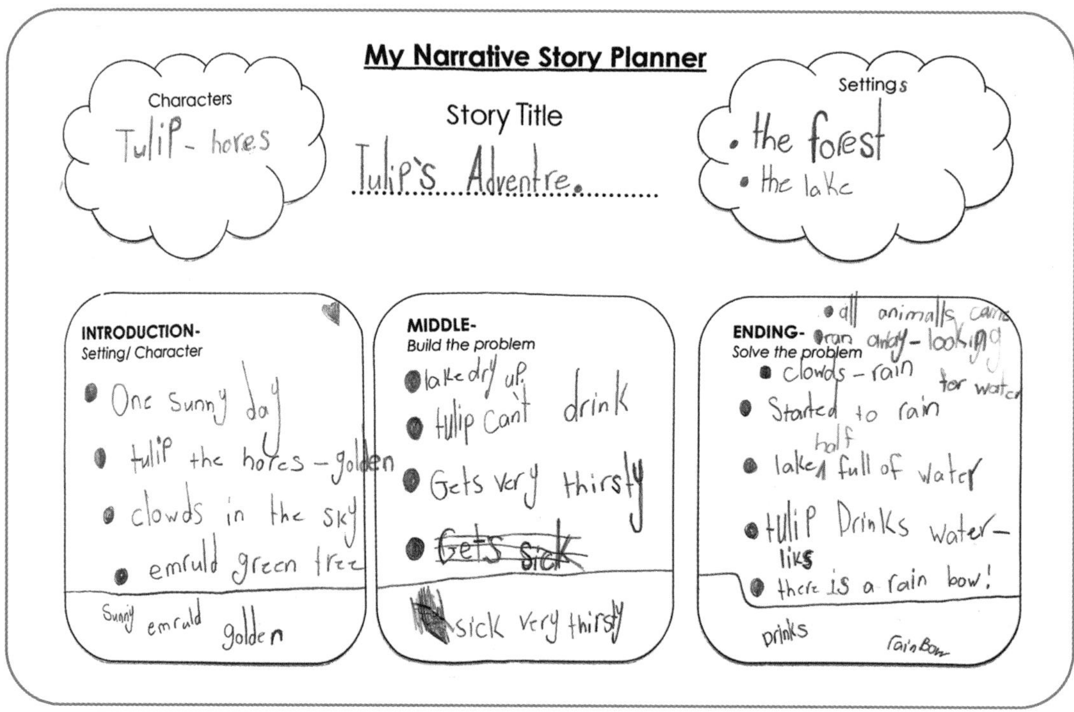

FIGURE 8.10 *Simple Graphic Organizer*

During the narrative writing unit, Tam was focused on providing student choice and differentiation to meet all the needs of her writers. Instead of giving only one graphic organizer as a planning option, Tam also introduced an additional graphic organizer for story planning. Figure 8.10 shows the work of a student who opted for the simpler version of the graphic organizer, which was introduced and practiced during reading instruction. However, Figure 8.11 shows the work of

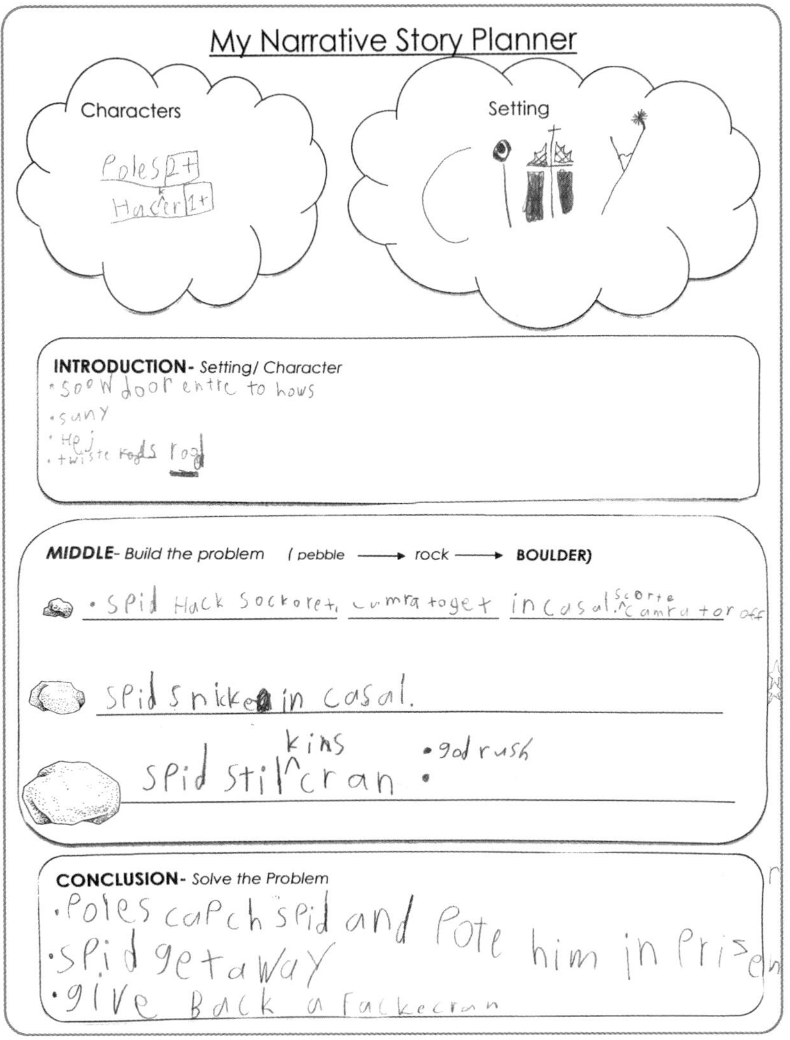

FIGURE 8.11 *Complex Graphic Organizer*

a student who opted for the more complex planner, which provided an expanded section for building up the problem. There is no perfect graphic organizer or preparation for student responses, so giving students choice and providing differentiated options can help students build confidence and academic success.

REFLECTION QUESTIONS

1. What resources do you currently prepare to support student responses?
2. What are some successes you have found with these resources?
3. What are some challenges you find with preparing resources for student responses?
4. What additional strategies for preparing resources for student responses have you seen?
5. How could you adapt one of these strategies to fit the needs of your multilingual students?

9 Prepare Structured Oral Language Opportunities with Talk-Equity Considerations

VIGNETTE

Bridgette had regularly been providing sentence stems and vocabulary support to assist her fourth-grade students in the early stages of English language proficiency. However, her multilingual students rarely raised their hands when she asked for a student to respond to her question or prompt. She reached out to her teaching teammates and voiced concern about how little some of her students were participating in oral language opportunities in her classroom. Her teammates felt similarly, so they set a goal to increase opportunities for student talk in their fourth-grade classrooms.

I was working with grade-level teams at this school to support teacher-driven inquiry and professional development related to supporting multilingual students. The teachers identified lack of oral language opportunities as their focal problem of practice. Together we designed and studied an intervention to address their goal of increasing productive student talk with a focus on equity for multilingual speakers. We asked ourselves: What is going well with oral language opportunities? What are some challenges? The teachers felt their preparation for student talk was a strength, such as visuals, sentence stems, and anchor charts. However, they felt the biggest challenge was the amount of designated time students had to talk in the literacy block and across the day.

We started by not changing anything the first week and doing an observational checklist about the number of students who spoke during the literacy period. At this point, we were not even concerned with the quality of talk; we simply wanted to know who was talking and how much they were talking. Monolingual students spoke significantly more than the multilingual students. A typical minilesson included three to four teacher questions and prompts with one to two students responding orally to each question. Many of the students performing at the lowest levels of English proficiency did not speak at all during the literacy period over the course of the week. The teachers were shocked when they realized the amount of talk students were completing during the literacy period because it was so low.

We brainstormed strategies that would help support more talk time, all of which you will see in this chapter. In addition to strategies, we also identified key priorities to deepen this work and make it more equitable for multilingual students. These priorities guided us in our instructional planning:

1. Create all questions and prompts to allow for student-to-student talk (eliminate the "one question with one student response" approach).
2. Continue support with sentence stems, word banks, vocabulary, and so on.
3. Provide extended, silent, uninterrupted wait time (no hand raising, no shouting out answers) to give multilingual students processing time for understanding the question and preparing a response.
4. Structure talk so that all students have the opportunity to talk and be the first person to talk. (For example, if we were planning a think-pair-share, we would plan a minimum of two instances. We would designate who went first with some criterion, such as

whose name came first in the alphabet. Then, for the second think-pair-share, the other partner would go first.)

Partner experiences have a huge return on talk time—if a teacher calls on one student after a prompt, that is something like one person out of thirty who gets the opportunity to speak. If students turn and talk, even if only one student in each pair talks, that is something like fifteen out of thirty people. With our plan of at least two partner talk experiences, this meant everyone had a structured oral language opportunity every day. We saw a huge increase in student talk, from an average of 10 percent of students talking one time in a literacy period to a minimum of 100 percent of students talking one time in a literacy period. Once this became a part of daily practice, the teachers began integrating additional structured oral language opportunities.

What Does the Research Say?

Extensive research documents the importance and benefits of providing opportunities for multilingual students to talk about content in pairs or small groups on a daily basis (Baker et al. 2014). Activities like the ones in this chapter, and specifically think-pair-share, have been shown to be helpful for processing content and practicing language (Lesaux et al. 2010). These oral language experiences provide multiple exposures to the language and opportunities to practice the language they are learning. Students can learn from each other, and the teacher can gain informal information about how well students are understanding new language and content (August et al. 2009).

Research has indicated that these experiences do not require extensive amounts of time, and students benefit from brief opportunities that occur multiple times a day (Echevarria, Vogt, and Short 2007). During these experiences, teachers should consider talk time equity, ensuring that all students get comparable amounts of talk time and opportunities. Additionally, it's particularly important to consider processing time equity for multilingual learners. As noted in Chapter 6, multiple studies have documented the benefits of providing wait time (Gambrell

1983; Hindman, Wasik, and Bradley 2018), particularly for multilingual students (Echevarria, Vogt, and Short 2007; Yaqubi and Rokni 2012). Appropriate scaffolds and wait time will help multilingual students be successful and gain the most benefit out of oral language opportunities.

Five Instructional Strategies

The key with all of these instructional strategies is planning ahead to ensure equitable access to oral language opportunities. This requires considerations for language proficiency and scaffolds that will be necessary for multilingual students to successfully participate. This will include strategies from previous chapters such as supports for academic vocabulary, processes, and resources for student responses.

Wait time is essential with the strategies in this chapter. Remember, the students will need time to process and possibly translate the initial instruction and content. Then, they will need time to process and possibly translate back to English how they will respond. This takes time, and it is terribly frustrating and discouraging to be deep in thought and hear other students shout out the answer before having a chance to prepare one. Wait time is probably the most overlooked scaffold, but it is powerful, free, and does not require any preparation.

The following instructional strategies and classroom examples build from the research on supporting oral language and the key equity considerations identified earlier.

STRATEGY 1 Think-Pair-Share for Multilingual Students

Teachers have been asking students to think, talk, and work with peers for a long time. However, some partner talk is more productive than others. Some educators found that simply telling students to talk to people near them did not produce the most productive and engaging talk. Because of this, educators and researchers have taken on many different forms of structuring partner talk. While some form of think-pair-share was likely used much earlier, the first published version of the strategy was written by Frank Lyman in 1981. This strategy is exactly what it sounds like: students think about a response, pair with a peer and discuss, and share the answer with the class.

Other educators have made modifications, such as Johnson, Johnson, and Smith's formulate-share-listen-create (1991). This strategy involves individually formulating an answer, sharing it with a partner, listening to and comparing responses with a partner, and creating a new answer based on both partners' ideas. Both of these can be effective strategies for supporting student talk.

For multilingual students, I adjust these strategies by displaying expectations and the talk prompt. I also provide sentence stems and vocabulary to support talk, along with extended wait time and planning for a minimum of two opportunities so that both partners get a chance to share their thinking first. You can see an example I did with a second-grade classroom working on identifying the author's message in Figure 9.1. Notice the visuals to reinforce the process. I introduced the talk prompt and language scaffolds or sentence stems. During the think time, I asked all students to get into the "thinker pose," where they would look forward and put their hand on their mouth to indicate they were thinking. During this time, there was no talking, hand raising, or movement until I told them it was time to pair. I also included how to decide who would talk first in my visually supported directions.

FIGURE 9.1 *Think-Pair-Share*

Steps for instruction

1. Identify an even number of open-ended talk prompts.
2. Create a slide or an anchor chart that includes the process (including who should talk first), talk prompt, and language supports.

3. Share the slide or anchor chart with students and provide silent and extended wait time.
4. Provide student talk time (some teachers use a timer and others keep it open ended).
5. Bring students back together and ask a few to share with the entire group.

STRATEGY 2 Think-Whisper–Let It Go for Multilingual Students

The think-whisper–let it go strategy is great because it includes 100 percent participation for student response. It involves the teacher posing a talk prompt or question, giving students time to think, having students whisper the answer into their hands, and then having everyone whisper or shout it out into the air in a choral response. I love this strategy because all students get a chance to respond in a low-stress situation because they are not singled out when using the choral response option.

Similar to my multilingual student version of think-pair-share, I have adjusted this strategy to include a visual representation of the process, written talk prompt, extended and silent wait time, and language scaffolds, as you can see in Figure 9.2.

Think . . .

How is the character feeling?

Whisper . . .

The character feels ______________________.

I think the character feels ______________________.

I think the character feels ______________________

because ______________________.

Let It Go . . .

Release your hands and let the answer out into the air.

FIGURE 9.2 *Think-Whisper–Let It Go*

For some groups, if the talk prompt is more extensive or they are going to share it in a small group, I will have them write their ideas down in a notebook first. This can help build confidence in providing more sophisticated responses. You can see an example of third graders whispering to rehearse their written responses in Figure 9.3.

FIGURE 9.3 *Whisper Rehearsal*

Steps for instruction

1. Create a talk prompt related to academic content and language.
2. Create a slide or an anchor chart that includes the process, talk prompt, and language supports.
3. Share the slide or anchor chart with students and provide silent and extended wait time.
4. Provide student whisper time (some teachers use a timer and others keep it open ended).
5. Ask students to chorally respond.

STRATEGY 3 Talking Chips for Multilingual Students

Everyone has been in a group or observed a group discussion where one or two people dominated the entire conversation. It can be difficult for other speakers to find a way in to the discussion. This is even more challenging for reluctant speakers and students learning a new language. The purpose of the talking chips strategy is to help prevent that challenge by equalizing the number of times each participant in the group can speak.

The basic premise of this strategy is that students in small groups will speak the same amount of times. Each student gets an equal number of chips (counting chips), and they place a chip in the center of the table every time they talk. Once a student runs out of chips, they cannot talk again until all other students have placed all their chips on the table (Kagan and Kagan 2009). Many educators have adapted this strategy, and it has taken on different forms in a variety of contexts. Some teachers give students only one to two chips each, while others might give as many as ten, depending on the activity. Some teachers use talking chips for very open-ended discussions such as book clubs, while others might use them for something like showing your work on math problems.

For multilingual students, I like this strategy because I can provide a wider range of differentiation options for participation than I can in a think-pair-share experience. I also like this strategy because while it does not fully mimic a natural conversation, it is much more natural than students taking turns answering questions based on whose name comes first in the alphabet. Both serve a purpose, but this strategy builds in talk equity with turn taking while also being a closer model for natural group discussion. The goal is that eventually students will not need these oral language structures and will independently have academic conversations in pairs and groups.

As with the previous strategies, I prioritize scaffolding the process and providing extended wait time and response scaffolds. I also draw on the resources from the previous chapter related to preparing scaffolds for student responses. Before I introduce the discussion prompt, I review a wide range of discussion sentence stems students can use. These can be as simple as "I agree with ________" for the beginning speakers or as complex as "The evidence for _______ is overwhelming when you consider that _______." Depending on the language proficiency level, I might also include key vocabulary with images to support their responses. You can easily modify this strategy for different topics, numbers of students, and numbers of responses.

Steps for instruction

1. Identify discussion topics or prompts that warrant extended conversation (multiple turn taking for each student in a small group).
2. Create a slide or an anchor chart that includes the process, talk prompt, and language supports (these might be a review of sentence stems for discussion).
3. Share the slide or anchor chart with students and provide silent and extended wait time to prepare for the conversation.
4. Place students in groups of three to six.
5. Provide student talk time (some teachers tell students to talk until they run out of chips; other teachers set a time frame, and when all students have used their chips, they collect them, start over again, and continue the discussion until time is up).
6. Bring students back together and ask a few to share with the entire group.

STRATEGY 4 Stand Up–Hand Up–Pair Up for Multilingual Students

Stand up–hand up–pair up (Kagan and Kagan 2009) is another cooperative learning structure that provides multiple opportunities for student talk. The strategy consists of posing a question or discussion prompt to students. Then, students stand up with their hand up in the air until they find a partner who does not sit in their table group. Once they have a partner, they begin a discussion, with each student sharing a response. Kagan and Kagan recommend setting a specific time limit for the discussion or sharing back-and-forth quick responses until the teacher calls time and then having students repeat the activity, typically with a new question or prompt.

I have made some adjustments to this strategy to better meet the needs of multilingual students. As mentioned in the previous strategies, I provide scaffolding for the process, talk prompt, extended wait time to prepare responses, sentence stems, and vocabulary. I want all of my students to have time to respond and do not want to add additional stress for language production. Because of this, I introduce the discussion prompt with scaffolds, provide wait time to prepare (sometimes I ask students to write their answer on a note card if I think it will be difficult to remember), and then I have them stand up with hands up until they find a partner.

However, instead of everyone waiting on a timer before finishing or moving to another partner, I tell students to complete the task, both talking at their own pace. Then, when they are ready, they can raise their hand again and find someone else with a hand raised and repeat the process. I encourage students to think about whether or not they would like to revise their original response for the second discussion based on what they heard from their first partner.

Students can continue moving at their own pace until the activity concludes. Unlike other versions of this scaffold, I have students share their same, or slightly modified, response, multiple times as they hear responses from multiple peers instead of talking about a new topic each time. This purposefully provides multiple exposures to peers' responses and an opportunity to build on and revise their response, build confidence, and feel successful. Typically, I give them about five minutes with a thirty-second countdown for the final share. Figure 9.4 is an example of a slide I used to introduce this oral language opportunity when students were studying theme.

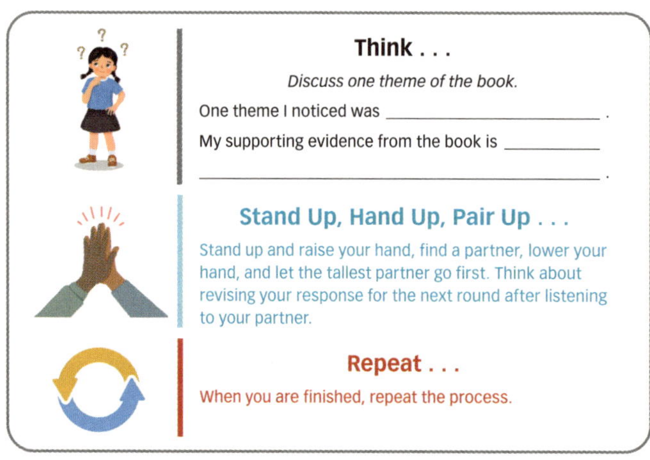

FIGURE 9.4 *Think–Stand Up–Hand Up–Pair Up*

Steps for instruction

1. Identify a discussion prompt related to academic content.
2. Create a slide or an anchor chart that includes the process, talk prompt, and language supports (these might be specific sentence stems or a review of general discussion sentence stems).
3. Share the slide or anchor chart with students and provide silent and extended wait time to prepare for the discussion. If needed, give students the option to write down their response.
4. Tell students to stand up, put their hands up, pair up, and begin discussion.
5. Set a timer.
6. Walk around the room to listen in on conversations and provide support if needed.

For students ready for a linguistic challenge, I adjust this strategy to be more complex to include both receptive and expressive challenges.

Steps for additional challenge

1. Identify a discussion prompt related to academic content.
2. Create a slide or an anchor chart that includes the process, talk prompt, and language supports (these might be specific sentence stems or a review of general discussion sentence stems).
3. Share the slide or anchor chart with students and provide silent and extended wait time to prepare for the discussion. If needed, give students the option to write down their response. Instead of revising and repeating their response, they will share their partner's response during the next round (see Figure 9.5).

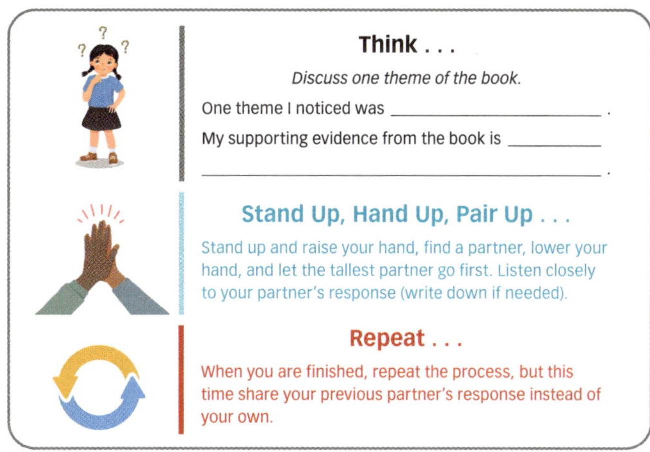

FIGURE 9.5 *Additional Challenge*

4. Tell students to stand up, put their hands up, and pair up.
5. Set a timer.
6. Walk around the room to listen in on conversations and provide support if needed.

STRATEGY 5 Oral Language Development Groups

In the literacy world, we talk a lot about small-group instruction. It is a way to provide differentiated support to meet the needs of students. Guided reading, literature discussion groups, strategy instruction groups, and word study groups are all common literacy-related forms of small-group instruction. However, most of these fail to take into consideration the needs of students learning a new language.

The most common hurdle I hear from teachers about providing instruction specifically targeted at oral language is time—with all the other requirements, where can they add in another subject? My solution to this is oral language development groups that have language development goals and instruction in coordination with literacy-related goals and instruction. This type of group is an opportunity to differentiate according to language and literacy needs.

To plan for these groups, I begin by analyzing my language proficiency data, specifically the oral language component. I look for students with a similar range of speaking proficiency to create groups. Then, I examine the reading assessment data for these students. I try to create groups of students where both the speaking proficiency and reading proficiency levels are similar, but there will always be a range and some groups that may have to be adjusted. For these groups, I am more concerned with the speaking proficiency being close.

These groups allow me to build on students' strengths in English reading and listening proficiency to provide supported speaking opportunities in low-stress situations. I develop two goals for these groups: literacy with language focus and oracy. I begin with literacy goals. These are directly related to the literacy content. This is the same objective I might have if I were not considering multilingual learners.

I often develop these objectives in connection with the literacy standards. For example, here's an initial literacy goal for an oral language small-group lesson I taught: students will make predictions and retell the story (this was directly related to the grade-level standard that was being addressed during whole-group instruction). Then I have to think about how I will scaffold this work with language considerations for multilingual learners.

The WIDA Can Do Descriptors goals are a great place to start to think about what multilingual learners *can* do (available on the WIDA website). The WIDA Can Do Descriptors guides are wonderful free resources that include grade-level bands with descriptors of what multilingual learners can do according to each stage of proficiency. I use these to help me plan for linguistically appropriate instruction and scaffolds. For example, based on my initial literacy goal and the speaking level (WIDA 2) of the students in my small oral language group, I went to the Can Do Descriptors and created the following goal for literacy with language focus: **predict** story content based on images and picture walk *using simple and expanded language frames*, and **retell** simple stories *from picture cues*. When I create such goals, I try to include the verb (or action) that students will do (in bold) as well as the scaffold or support that I will provide to assist students in this process (in italics).

Oracy goals are based on considerations for dialogue, vocabulary, and language structures (Escamilla et al. 2014). These components help me think about the specifics of language learning and development beyond just proficiency levels. Dialogue considerations could be related to a focus on open-ended questions, connected discourse, problem-solving, and so on (Escamilla et al. 2014). Vocabulary considerations should include a focus on refining and expanding in meaningful ways, not decontextualized memorization. Language structures can focus on a variety of aspects, but Figure 9.6 provides some sample goals related to language structures.

For the example I mentioned earlier, I created the following oracy goals based on what was linguistically appropriate for students' proficiency level:

Goal	Example
Expand grammatical complexity	› Expand statements using connected discourse › Simple sentences › Prepositions › Conjunctions › Relative pronouns
Provide opportunity for transformations	› Statements to questions › Positive to negative statements › Questions to statements › Requests to commands › Statements to exclamations
Forms and functions	› Language to address various communicative tasks (e.g., agree or disagree, make a request, compare and contrast

Adapted from Gentile (2004) and Escamilla et al. (2014).

FIGURE 9.6 *Goals*

1. Children will practice changing questions to answers and expanding grammatical complexity (temporal and tense changes in evolving predictions).
2. Children will use pictures to guide a retelling and use new vocabulary.

I create and use an observational note-taking guide for informal assessment purposes and to inform my future instruction. Figure 9.7 is an example of the one I created and used for this lesson (see OR 9–1 in the Online Resources for a blank version). I can take notes about the literacy-related goals and make a check mark when the student demonstrates the oracy goal. It is easy to update the guide for future lessons by changing the literacy and oracy goals in the guide.

Then I use the following process to teach the oral language development group with high-quality, high-interest, and culturally relevant children's literature. There are more practice stages in this type of lesson than in a typical I do–we do–you do structure because the goal is for students to have as many opportunities as possible to practice speaking and applying what they learned to reach the language and literacy goals.

1. *Modeling:* The teacher connects to prior learning, introduces the vocabulary, and models the oracy and literacy goals with scaffolds.
2. *Shared practice:* The teacher invites students to practice the oracy and literacy goals with a partner while the teacher supports.
3. *Interactive practice:* During the reading of the book (could be echo, choral, or teacher read, depending on level), the teacher stops at points for students to work with partners to practice the oracy and literacy goals, encouraging use of previously introduced vocabulary. The teacher encourages students to help each other, as opposed to just taking turns.

OR 9–1

TRACKING GOALS

Group: ______________________ Date: ______________

SMALL-GROUP BOOK AND INSTRUCTIONAL FOCUS: *Alma and How She Got Her Name*

› ***Goal as related to can-do descriptors:*** **Predict** story content based on images and picture walk using simple and expanded language frames; **retell** simple stories from picture cues.

› ***Oracy objective:*** Children will learn how to change questions to answers and practice expanding grammatical complexity (temporal and tense changes); use pictures to guide retelling and use new vocabulary.

› ***Oracy considerations:*** language structures, vocabulary, dialogue

› ***Notes and ideas for next meeting:*** Students showed strong predicting skills but needed more support for accurate and detailed retell for 2/5. Use of new vocabulary was limited, so will need to revisit to reinforce independent use. 5/5 changing question to answer with support, will need to revisit and reinforce temporal and tense changes.

Name	Can-Do Goal Predict	Can-Do Goal Retell	Oracy (circle oracy objectives students meet)
Karla	Strong and related prediction	Short, missing problem	Change question to answer. (circled) Expand grammatical complexity. Use vocab.
Jon	Accurate prediction with supporting evidence	Really long, overly detailed retell	Change question to answer. (circled) Expand grammatical complexity. Use vocab.
Emilio	Prediction using images and title	Brief retell	Change question to answer. (circled) Expand grammatical complexity. Use vocab.
Mei	Accurate prediction with supporting reasoning	Accurate retell with beginning, middle, and end (used vocab)	Change question to answer. (circled) Expand grammatical complexity. Use vocab. (circled)
Paloma	Strong prediction based on picture walk	Strong retell	Change question to answer. (circled) Expand grammatical complexity. Use vocab.

FIGURE 9.7 *Note-Taking Guide* OR 9-1

4. *Independent practice:* At the completion of reading, the teacher asks the students to independently demonstrate the literacy- and language-related goals. Depending on the goal, this may require teacher questioning or prompts. Students will share their independent response with a partner.
5. *Collaborative reinforcement and feedback:* Students listen to their peers and provide feedback. This gives students an audience for their oral language practice, helps them think more deeply about the language and the task, and offers an opportunity for listening and responding to academic tasks. For oral language groups, I typically use two requirements with sentence stems to scaffold the feedback to include positive acknowledgment and possible suggestions. Students listen to the speaker and then respond with the following two comments: "I really like ________," and "I might add [or change] ________."

Steps for instruction

1. Analyze language proficiency data and literacy proficiency data.
2. Use the data to group students by oral language proficiency needs.
3. If multiple groups are needed, group according to literacy proficiency data and needs.
4. Create literacy-related goals with a language focus based on students' oral language proficiency level.
5. Create oracy goals based on their oral language proficiency level.
6. Prepare the observational note-taking guide.
7. Teach the small group using the following process: modeling, shared practice, interactive practice, independent practice, and collaborative reinforcement and feedback.
8. Encourage students to connect their learning to future conversations and literacy learning.

Strategies in Action: Intermediate-Grade Resources to Support Student Response

Cat Frayne, a third-grade teacher at the Columbus School in Medellín, Colombia, wanted to increase student engagement and productive academic talk during book clubs with her multilingual students. She noticed some students were dominating the conversations while others were mostly listening. Cat learned about the talking chips strategy in a professional development workshop, but she felt it did not do enough to support focused conversations that used academic language and applied literacy content from whole-group instruction. She noticed some students would just contribute a chip and respond with a basic statement like "I agree with you" instead of pushing themselves to use academic language and a variety of ways of responding.

Cat created a new version of talking chips that included supports for the number of times students could talk *and* the types of talk they would use. Cat introduced response options with sentence stems for questions, comments, and connections, as you can see in Figure 9.8 (see also OR 9–2 in the Online Resources).

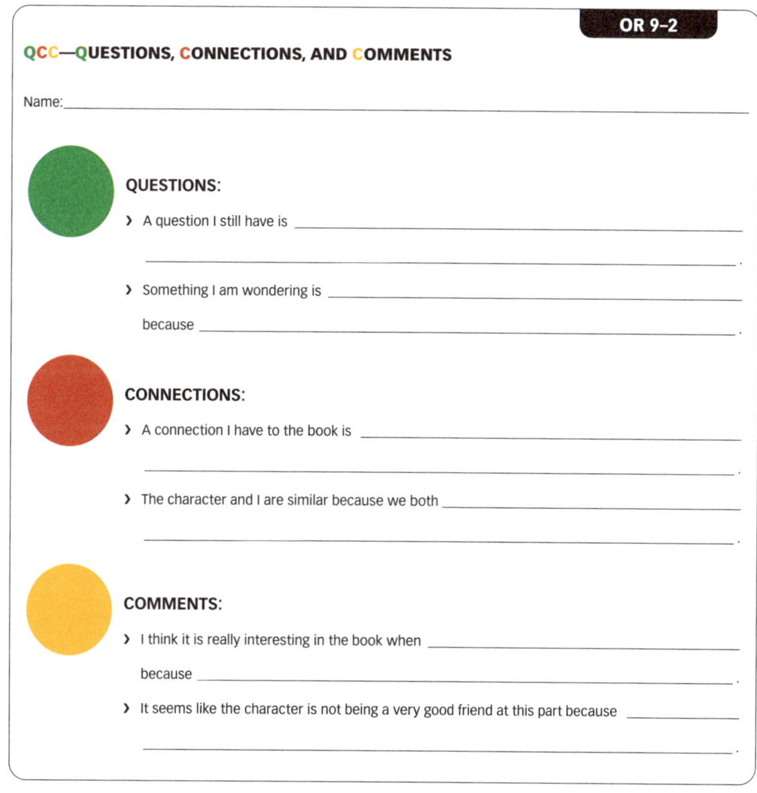
OR 9–2

QCC—QUESTIONS, CONNECTIONS, AND COMMENTS

Name: ______________________

QUESTIONS:

› A question I still have is ______________________ .

› Something I am wondering is ______________________ because ______________________ .

CONNECTIONS:

› A connection I have to the book is ______________________ .

› The character and I are similar because we both ______________________ .

COMMENTS:

› I think it is really interesting in the book when ______________________ because ______________________ .

› It seems like the character is not being a very good friend at this part because ______________________ .

FIGURE 9.8 *Talking Chips for Questions, Connections, and Comments* OR 9-2

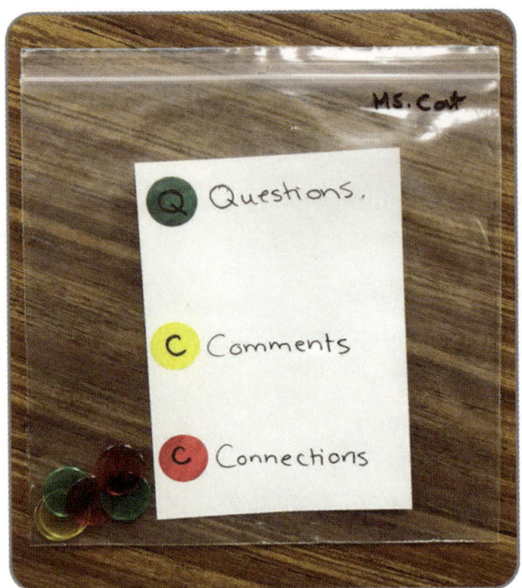

FIGURE 9.9 *Questions, Comments, and Connections Book Bag*

This provided a strong support for options for interactions. However, Cat wanted students to respond using all three approaches, not just one, so she designed a color-coded version of talking chips. The students got their book club book in a bag with colored chips and a corresponding graphic organizer to use when participating in the discussion (see Figure 9.9). They had fifteen minutes for book club. During that time, students needed to ask two questions, make two connections, and add two comments to the conversation. They did not need to complete these in any specific order, and Cat encouraged them to use the chips to make the conversation flow naturally. Once everyone used all their chips, they collected them and continued the conversation, each with a full set of chips. The students loved it because they had a lot of chips, which gave them freedom to respond to their peers in different ways.

I was fortunate to listen in on one of the book clubs, and I loved the range of ways students used this scaffold. Some students strictly used the sentence stems and did not veer much beyond them, and other students expanded on the sentence stems and added multiple other sentences. I heard a student ask a question about vocabulary, and another responded with a comment with a child-friendly definition and the translation in Spanish. Then, another student added a connection to the meaning of the word in a current news story. In this same group, one student had not contributed much, so another student said, "José, you still have a lot of chips. Do you want to use one?" The students had a concrete way to keep track of who was talking and what types of talk were happening or missing. They used this to support each other and move the conversation forward in engaging ways, as shown in Figure 9.10.

FIGURE 9.10 *Students Engaging with QCC Talking Chips*

REFLECTION QUESTIONS

1. What types of oral language opportunities do your students currently have?
2. What are some successes you have found with supporting oral language opportunities?
3. What are some challenges you find with supporting oral language opportunities?
4. What talk-equity considerations could you add to your oral language opportunities to better support your multilingual students?
5. How could you use and adapt one or more of these strategies to fit the needs of your multilingual students?

Connect to and Build on Students' Home Language Skills and Knowledge

VIGNETTE

The following anecdotes highlight two misconceptions related to connecting to and building on students' home language skills and knowledge.

> *Misconception: Parents should speak only in English with their children at home.*

A parent whose primary language was Mandarin came to the teacher worried about how to help their intermediate-age child at home: "I try to only speak English, but there are a lot of words and things I don't know in English, so it is hard. I tell him, 'No Mandarin books or shows, only English,' but I know he is reading online in Mandarin and talking with his friends in Mandarin. I don't know how to help him."

The teacher, who was also a specialist in second language development, responded: "Actually, the research now shows us that proficiency in students' home language supports development in an additional language. Talking, reading, and thinking with your child at home in Mandarin will also help support the work we are doing in school in English. It is also so very important that your child maintains proficiency in Mandarin, his home language."

> *Misconception: Teachers who do not speak the home language of children cannot connect to and build on students' home language skills and knowledge.*

Mel, a teacher new to teaching multilingual students, confessed to her mentor after the back-to-school professional development day on supporting multilingual students: "I feel unprepared. So many of you speak Spanish, or at least a little Spanish, but I don't. I don't see how I can build on students' home language when I don't know the home language. I am really worried that I won't be able to do what the school is asking and that my students will suffer because I only speak English."

Mel's mentor reassured her. "Of course, it makes it easier if you speak students' home language, but one year I had eight different home languages in my classroom. The key in this work is finding resources to support but also recognizing that students are knowledgeable and have a whole host of resources they bring to class. They might not yet be able to communicate that in English, but it is our job to find ways to build on what they know, make connections to their home language, and build on it. The online resources are getting better every day. I can share some of the tools I use to help become more knowledgeable about students' home languages and how I use them to better support the students."

What Does the Research Say?

Building on students' home language skills has been documented as a beneficial practice by many scholars (August, Fenner, and Snyder 2014; Cook 2001; Goldenberg 2013). Leveraging students' bilingualism can promote academic, cognitive, and social achievement growth (Cummins 2005). More recently, a great deal of research has been conducted on translanguaging pedagogies and practices in the classroom (Goodman and Tastanbek 2021; Wei 2018; Moses and Capurro 2023). Translanguaging is a process in which people draw on all of their linguistic resources, utilizing multiple languages (García 2020). Using translanguaging in instruction is a powerful tool to support multilinguals in accessing content. Translanguaging as a pedagogical strategy is frequently discussed in bilingual contexts, but supporting student translanguaging in thinking, planning, collaborating, and documenting learning is equally as important.

One approach to translanguaging pedagogy is spontaneous translanguaging. This is where students or teachers use multiple languages to learn, clarify, explain, or translate to each other in the moment as needed. The other approach that will be present in the examples in this chapter is planned and strategic use of multiple languages to draw on students' knowledge base across languages during the input, processing, and output stages of learning. Strategic translanguaging in classrooms can provide benefits such as helping learners access background knowledge (Sayer 2013), assisting with metalinguistic awareness (Jiménez et al. 2015), and supporting vocabulary development (Cunningham and Graham 2000).

Five Instructional Strategies

As mentioned in the vignette, it is easier to do these strategies if you speak the home language of your students. However, it is *not* a requirement. Modeling vulnerability, learning a language, and showing students you care enough to try to connect to their strengths and home language go a long way in building community and confidence. The online resources for this type of work are improving at a rapid rate, and many are free. There is the traditional Google Translate™ application, which now translates speech, text, and images for 133 languages. Apple Translate, SpeakText, Microsoft Translator, BK Translate, SayHi Translate, iTranslate, and Linguee are all free translation apps. Artificial intelligence resources are becoming more and more helpful not only with translation but also with some explanations and contrastive analysis between languages, as I discuss in the "Strategies in Action" section. None of them is perfect or better than a person who's proficient in the language, but they are great resources and can provide a lot of support if you don't speak the language.

STRATEGY 1 Find, Use, and Read Translanguaging Books

Translingual books are a wonderful way to model published authors' translanguaging practices for students. The number of books containing the integration of multiple languages that are not just directly translated but infuse more than one language throughout the text, dialogue, and pictures is growing. Many of these books also include a pronunciation guide or bilingual glossary to help support monolingual speakers. The website Libros for Language has created an extensive list and categorized various translanguaging text types across a range of languages and grade levels.

While reading aloud for enjoyment is always a wonderful option, I encourage using these texts to also draw attention to language choice, author identity, and translanguaging options and positive identity development for multilingual students (Moses, Hajdun, and Aguirre 2021). I recommend reading a translanguaging book for the first time for joy and exposure. During the second read, I prompt students to notice the different uses of languages throughout the book. Then, we discuss and categorize the types of words used in different languages before we talk about the author's purpose for and strategic use of multiple languages. Finally, I encourage students to think about how, when, and for what purposes they can use multiple languages in their daily lives and writing.

Steps for instruction

1. Find high-quality translanguaging books that are culturally and linguistically relevant to your students.
2. Prepare for the read-aloud by reading the text and identifying unknown words or pronunciation of words. If there is not a pronunciation guide or glossary, look the words and pronunciation up online to ensure accurate reading and representation of both languages.
3. Read the story aloud for enjoyment with the students.

4. Tell the students you are going to reread this book written by a bilingual author who uses multiple languages throughout.
5. Ask them to be thinking about and noticing the use of different languages throughout the book.
6. With student input, stop and jot down words that are written in the language other than English.
7. Ask students to work with partners to discuss and categorize the words in the language other than English.
8. Have students share with the class.
9. Ask students to work in pairs to discuss their noticings about what content was in English and what content was in the language other than English.
10. Have students share with the class.
11. Ask students to discuss the author's purpose and strategic use of multiple languages.
12. Have students share with the class.
13. Encourage students to think about how, when, and for what purposes they can use multiple languages.

STRATEGY 2 Introduce and Draw Attention to Cognates

Cognates are words that share the same linguistic derivation and have identical or nearly identical spellings and meanings. For example, the English word *perfect* and the Spanish word *perfecto* both mean "as good as possible" or "free from faults." Another example: the word *banque* in French means the same as *bank* in English. Introducing and drawing attention to cognates can provide access to comprehension of a large number of words without any formal definition, instruction, or memorization. This is particularly true with Spanish and English. Thirty to 40 percent of all English words have a related Spanish word (Calderón et al. 2003). Teaching students about cognates and to look for cognates taps into their rich linguistic knowledge and helps them better connect to and learn academic language in English.

Teachers approach cognate teaching in many different ways. Teaching and using morphology to recognize cognates can be particularly helpful. For example, teaching Greek and Latin prefixes, root words, and suffixes that are similar across languages can provide access to and understanding of so many words. See Figures 10.1 and 10.2 for an example of how Matt Hajdun, Cat Frayne, and Dana Cheriff introduced some of these patterns.

When Dana introduced cognates, she created a class cognate tree and encouraged students to help her add to it as they discovered new cognates in their reading or conversations (see Figure 10.3).

In both languages, we can break words into parts to determine their meaning. English and Spanish share parts of words from Latin and Greek. The word parts can have the same meaning in both languages and help us solve new words.

Bridge 6: Common Roots

bio	graph	y
bio	*graf*	*ía*
life	**write**	

FIGURE 10.1 *Morphology and Cognates Slide 1*

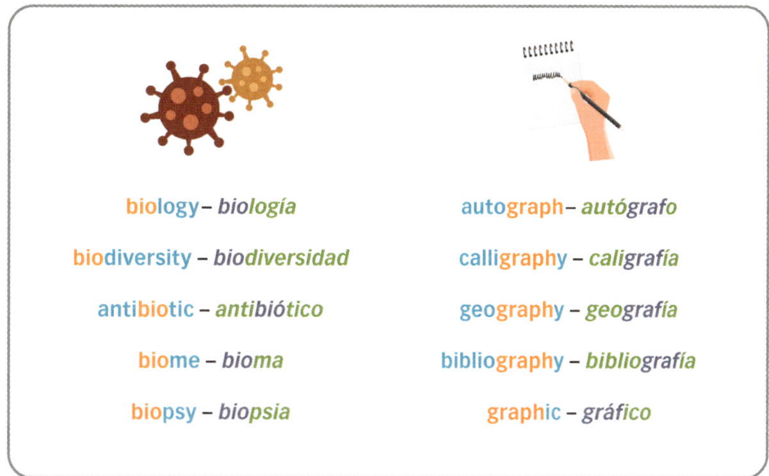

FIGURE 10.2 *Morphology and Cognates Slide 2*

Dana and her students also identified false cognates (words that look similar but mean different things), for example, *embarrassed* and *embarazada* (pregnant).

I have seen cognate work done with two different approaches. One was an inquiry-based approach where the teacher asked for

FIGURE 10.3 *Cognate Tree*

student input when reading to try to find cognates or morpheme connections across languages. The other was teacher directed, with a specific focus on words and morphemes related to the reading content.

Steps for a teacher-directed approach

1. Identify prefixes, root words, or suffixes from the upcoming reading or unit that would work well with the cognate morphology strategy (connect across the languages).
2. Explain to students what cognates are with multiple examples.
3. Model identifying morphemes in English, for example, *bio-graph-y*.
4. Model identifying morphemes in the other language. For example, *bio-graf-ía*.
5. Explicitly teach the meaning of the morphemes and compare across languages.

6. Provide a list of cognates with the prefix, root word, or suffix you introduced. Highlight the cognate morphology.
7. Encourage students to look for cognates and add to a cognate tree.

Steps for an inquiry-based approach

1. Explain to students what cognates are and give multiple examples.
2. Model identifying morphemes in English, for example: *bio-graph-y*.
3. Ask students if they can identify any morphemes in their home language that are similar.
4. Ask students to help you generate a list of cognates with the prefix, root word, or suffix you introduced. Highlight the cognate morphology.
5. Encourage students to look for cognates and add to a cognate tree.

STRATEGY 3 Use Bilingual Resources

Bilingual resources are a great way to connect to and build on students' knowledge in their home language. These resources can mean the difference between participating and having access to learning and sharing and having no idea what is happening for beginning speakers. With all the technology tools that are available for free, teachers can create these resources regardless of their language proficiency in other languages. I always fear using these tools because they might have mistakes or inaccuracies in the translation. However, I have used this as a way to model learning, vulnerability, and looking to my students to be the experts in their home language. I encourage them to tell me, in a polite way, if something I created or had translated is not accurate. I am honest and clear about wanting to learn their language but not being able to do it yet without the support of these tools and their knowledge. This creates a space of shared expertise.

Bilingual resources can take on many forms, and they can be used by the teacher during instruction or by the students during practice. Bilingual books (with two versions of the story in the book in

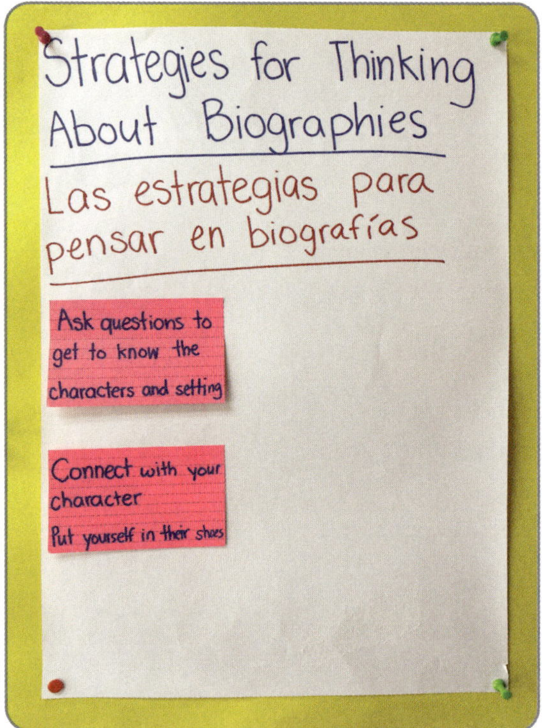

FIGURE 10.4 *Bilingual Anchor Chart*

two languages) or sets of books in different languages are common resources often found in the school or local library. Other resources might include bilingual dictionaries, bilingual anchor charts, bilingual labels, bilingual vocabulary cards, bilingual word banks, bilingual word lists, and bilingual word walls. You can adapt bilingual resources depending on the instructional focus and student needs. Providing even a small amount of bilingual support for key strategies or anchor charts that the class will revisit, as in Dana Cheriff's chart in Figure 10.4, can be extremely helpful for multilingual students.

Teachers often create these resources to support a unit or topic that students will be learning about over time. I wanted to create an easy bilingual resource for the fourth graders I was working with on character traits in Brazil. I knew they would be revisiting character traits throughout the unit, so I asked students to paste this into their reading notebooks and add to it as they identified new words for character traits. (See Figure 10.5.) I do not speak Portuguese, so I used ChatGPT to support this process. I told ChatGPT to create an English-to-Portuguese bilingual list of character traits. It produced a list. Then, I told it to put the information into a chart. I used that chart to create the list in Figure 10.5.

You could also use this process to make a bilingual word wall to display in the class during the unit. Students could add to it as they identified additional character traits in both languages. Additionally, it is easy to tell ChatGPT to add languages to the chart if there are more than two languages spoken in the classroom.

English	Portuguese
honest	honesto/a
brave	corajoso/a
kind	amável
generous	generoso/a
compassionate	compassivo/a
ambitious	ambicioso/a
confident	confiante
patient	paciente
responsible	responsável
empathetic	empático/a
loyal	leal
humble	humilde
optimistic	otimista
creative	criativo/a
trustworthy	confiável
caring	carinhoso/a
resilient	resiliente
cooperative	cooperativo/a
curious	curioso/a
determined	determinado/a
friendly	amigável
tolerant	tolerante
polite	educado/a
selfless	altruísta
understanding	compreensivo/a
reliable	confiável
adventurous	aventureiro/a
thoughtful	atencioso/a
grateful	grato/a

FIGURE 10.5 *Character Traits Bilingual List*

Steps for instruction

1. Identify key language that students will need to know to understand instruction and document their learning (vocabulary, sentence stems, sentences, instructions, responses, etc.).
2. Decide which bilingual resource format would be most helpful for your instructional goals.
3. If you are fluent in both languages, you can translate and create resources yourself.
4. If you are not fluent in both languages, use a translation tool or AI to help you translate the key material you identified.
5. Create the resource and model how to use it (word bank, word wall, list, etc.).
6. Make sure to model for students that you used the technology tool or resources to support your translation. Tell them you are learning and there might be errors, so you will benefit from their expertise if they see an error.
7. Continue reinforcement of using the resource and extending language use during writing and discussions.

STRATEGY 4 Perform Contrastive Analysis

Contrastive analysis is the study and comparison of two languages. Contrastive analysis helps language learners better understand a new language by building on their knowledge in the first language. It assists language learners in identifying common linguistic patterns that are similar and different across languages. A familiar and common example of this is comparing adjective and noun placement in English and in Spanish. In English, the adjective precedes the noun (*the red ball*). In Spanish, the noun precedes the adjective (*la pelota roja*).

These simple noticings are a great start but they get more sophisticated quickly with students' language development. It is helpful if the teacher has background knowledge about students' home languages.

However, it is very possible to do this work even if the teacher does not have a lot of background knowledge in the language. A quick internet search about similarities or common mistakes across the two languages will give some helpful initial information. Additionally, a quick chatbot search of common language differences and similarities between the two languages will give you information about vocabulary, grammar, pronunciation, verb tenses, articles, and much more. As mentioned in previous chapters, teachers do not have to know it all. They can model not knowing and asking students or bilingual experts for help. They can analyze the language alongside children and learn together in addition to doing some online research. Creating an analytical approach to thinking about language is equally as important as any individual analysis of a rule or structural pattern.

As with vocabulary instruction and grammar instruction, I encourage teachers to connect contrastive analysis to text and content the students are learning. For example, Matt Hajdun created a series of eight bridging lessons where he introduced students to a contrastive analysis teaching point that would be particularly helpful when reading and writing in a biography unit. Figure 10.6 is the slide he used to introduce the contrastive analysis about using superlatives in English and in Spanish. The slides also included examples from the books the students were reading in English and in Spanish.

In English, you can add a suffix to some words to make the superlative. In Spanish, you always add *más* before the word. Normally, in Spanish, the adjective comes after the noun, but in both English and Spanish the superlative adjective *best/mejor* comes before the noun.

Bridge 1: Using Superlatives

English	Español	Example from Text
the youngEST the kindEST the bravEST --------- **the most** famous **the most** thoughtful --------- **the best** singer **the best** player	**el/la más** joven **el/la más** amable **el/la más** valiente --------- **el más** famoso **la más** reflexivo --------- **la mejor** cantante **el mejor** jugador	

FIGURE 10.6 *Contrastive Analysis*

Steps if the teacher knows both languages

1. Identify key structures that contrastive analysis would provide support for when reading and writing in this unit or lesson.
2. Plan a brief bridging lesson to draw attention to similarities or differences between languages.
3. Create a slide or an anchor chart that includes a brief description of the structure you are teaching or drawing attention to in the contrastive analysis. Include examples in both languages side by side as well as examples from the texts students will be reading.
4. Provide brief instruction with the slide.
5. Ask students to share any other examples they know.
6. Encourage students to look for this in their reading and think about how to use it in their writing.
7. Create a wall or resource where students can contribute and add contrastive analysis when they encounter examples in their reading.

Steps if the teacher does not know both languages

1. Work with bilingual support in the building and do some online research to plan bridging lessons. Students can help support and explore with you.
2. If that is not possible, create a simple bridging lesson by doing a simple online search or using a chatbot.
3. Create a slide or an anchor chart that includes a brief description of the structure you are teaching or drawing attention to in the contrastive analysis. Include examples in both languages side by side as well as examples from the texts students will be reading.
4. Provide short instruction with the slide and explain that you are also learning how the other language works, so everyone in the class is sharing expertise.
5. Ask students to share any other examples they know.
6. Encourage students to look for this in their reading and think about how to use it in their writing.

7. Create a wall or resource where students can contribute and add contrastive analysis when they encounter examples in their reading.

STRATEGY 5 Use Multilingual Small Reading Groups

One of the biggest challenges, particularly in the older grades, is making sure students have access to grade-level content, thinking, skills, and concepts. Regardless of multilingual students' language proficiency levels, they are developmentally ready for deeper levels of thinking, critique, and analysis in reading. This is difficult to do with simple and vocabulary-controlled texts designed for speakers in the beginning three levels of language proficiency.

Because of this, I often use multilingual small groups for reading in the older grades when students are performing in the first three levels of English proficiency. I have the students independently read the text in their strongest language, but the group lesson, discussion, and output are completed in English. This works easily with strategy instruction groups or literature discussion groups.

For literature discussion groups, I give students guiding questions or broad topics for discussion prior to reading. Beginning speakers can translate the questions, if needed, prior to reading. This helps guide their thinking and prepare them for how they will contribute to the discussion in English when the group meets. All students read the book in their strongest language and prepare brief notes to help guide discussion. As noted in earlier chapters, students also have sentence stems to help guide discussion groups. The group comes together and discusses the reading in English.

Strategy instruction groups are organized according to student need, not level. The teacher observes a need (skill, strategy, etc.) for some students in the class and creates a small group to address this need. The teacher models and teaches the needed skill or strategy, tells students why it is important, and then asks students to practice it in a book they are independently reading. Instead of having everyone practice in the same book, this allows students to practice the strategy in a text that is at an appropriate level for them. The teacher coaches and provides support while they practice. Students and teachers share examples at the end and discuss using this strategy in future reading.

For example, five fourth-grade students were struggling to infer character motive and provide supporting evidence for their inferences. The students had a wide range of language and reading proficiency levels. However, they all had the same skills-based need. Three of the students were monolingual English speakers, one student spoke French as a first language, and the other student spoke Spanish as a first language. I asked them all to bring a book they had been reading during independent reading time. I specifically asked the French and Spanish speakers to bring one they were currently reading in their first language.

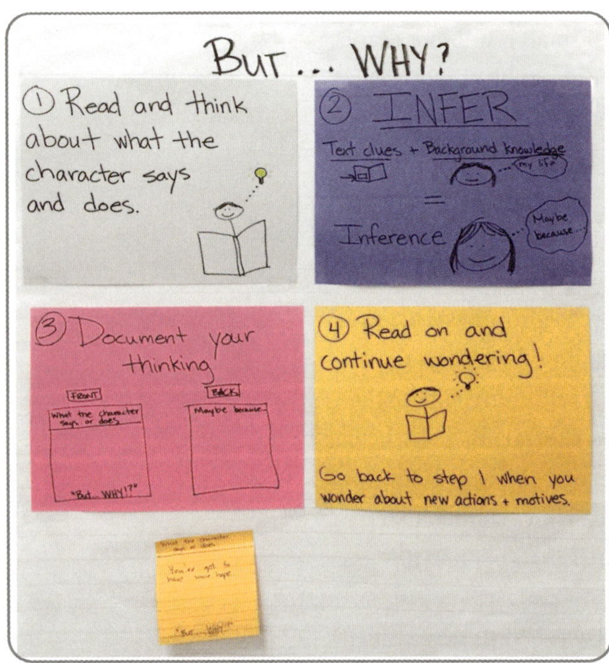

FIGURE 10.7 *"But . . . Why?" Strategy Chart*

I explained the importance of inferring the character motives and using background knowledge and clues from the text to better understand the plot development. I modeled step-by-step with a book we had been reading as a whole class, using the anchor chart adapted from Serravallo's *The Reading Strategies Book* (2015) in Figure 10.7. Then, I gave students a sticky note and asked them to try the strategy in the book they had been reading. The sticky notes had scaffolds written on them ("What the character says and does," "But . . . WHY?" and "Maybe because . . ."). I encouraged them to write on the sticky note in English so we could discuss together. They all tried it, and they shared their sticky note and thinking with a partner in English. I encouraged them to continue practicing this strategy when reading in the first language and in English. This allowed all students to read complex texts and apply and reinforce a comprehension strategy, regardless of their language proficiency. The goal was strategy support, so being able to read in their first language allowed them access to grade-level thinking and strategy use that they would not have been able to use in a simple beginning-level English text.

Steps for literature discussion groups

1. Find high-interest text sets in multiple languages.
2. Create small groups of students to read the same text.
3. Draw on strategies from previous chapters to prepare students for discussions (sentence stems, interactive patterns, etc.).
4. Prepare guiding questions or broad topics for discussion and give to students prior to reading.
5. Students read the text in their strongest language.
6. Students take notes to prepare for discussion in English.
7. Students come together and have a literature discussion in English (as much as possible).

Steps for strategy instruction groups

1. Identify students with the same instructional need, regardless of language or literacy proficiency level.
2. Prepare for student practice (gather sticky notes, prepare sentence stems, prepare anything that students will need to support their independent practice).
3. Tell students to bring a book they are reading independently in their strongest language to the small group.
4. Teach a lesson to introduce or reinforce a previously introduced strategy that will address the identified need. State the purpose and then model the strategy in a familiar text.
5. Ask students to practice the strategy with a book they are independently reading in their strongest language. Tell them that they will be sharing their strategy usage in English.

6. Coach students as needed while they are applying and documenting their strategy use.
7. Have students share with partners or the group.
8. Connect strategy learning to future reading in both languages.

Strategies in Action: Primary-Grade Strategies for Connecting to Students' Home Languages

Many of the instructional strategies for drawing on students' home language requires preparation. Previously, this type of work and translating could take hours. Sarah, an international literacy strategist, provides professional development related to literacy instruction at international schools around the world and has been exploring how she can use AI to help cut down on her planning time. In the following anecdote you can see she used it in three ways: translating lists and sentence stems into the various languages used in the class, gaining information about grammar to inform her instruction, and getting information and translated examples to prepare a contrastive analysis.

Sarah was preparing for a model lesson in a first-grade classroom in Vietnam. The class was already deeply immersed in word recognition, but they wanted to see Sarah teach a demonstration lesson on oral language development, vocabulary review, and expanding students' sentences. Sarah used ChatGPT to help prepare for the lesson. She first identified vocabulary words that centered on the human body, a focus in the grade one classroom. She pulled these words from the mentor text glossaries that the grade level was using. Sarah then told ChatGPT to take the list and create a new table for the languages represented in the class, and it translated them all. She also had it translate the sentence frame "My _______ is connected to my _______" into Vietnamese, the main home language in the classroom. Having these multilingual resources prepared in advance (and in only minutes) would be a valuable resource for students.

Plurals in Vietnamese and Korean work differently from English. Here's an overview of how pluralization works in these two languages:

Vietnamese:

In Vietnamese, plurals are usually not indicated by adding suffixes or separate words as in English. The number of items is often determined by the context, word order, or specific quantifiers. Here are some key points to understand plurals in Vietnamese:

1. **Context**: Vietnamese often relies on the context to convey whether something is singular or plural. For example, "Cái bàn" means "the table," while "Cái bàn kia" means "those tables."
2. **Quantifiers**: Specific quantifiers can be used to indicate the quantity of objects. For example, "một" means "one," "hai" means "two," and so on.
3. **Reduplication**: In some cases, reduplication of a noun or classifier can indicate plurality. For example, "bàn bàn" might be used to mean "tables" or "a lot of tables."
4. **Classifiers**: Vietnamese uses classifiers or measure words that come before the noun to specify the quantity. For example, "con" can be used with animals, "chiếc" with objects, and "người" with people.

FIGURE 10.8 *Artificial Intelligence Language Support*

In preparation for expanding students' sentences, she asked ChatGPT to explain to her the grammar behind the possessive pronouns as well as the conjunction *so* to expand on their ideas. Finally, she asked ChatGPT to explain how plurals work in Vietnamese and Korean so the students could do a contrastive analysis during the *-es* lesson. She used the information in Figure 10.8 to guide a contrastive analysis with students' home language and English. Using AI provided quick translations, grammar information, and contrastive analysis information across multiple languages to help Sarah prepare for instruction that would meet the students' needs.

REFLECTION QUESTIONS

1. What types of opportunities to connect to and build on students' home language do your students currently have?
2. What are some successes you have found with connecting to and building on students' home language?
3. What are some challenges you find with connecting to and building on students' home language?
4. What strategies could you add to your literacy instruction to better support your multilingual students?
5. How could you adapt one or more of these strategies to fit the needs of your multilingual students?

11

Draw Attention to Language and Expanding Grammatical Complexity

VIGNETTE

Grammar is a surprisingly polarizing topic in literacy education and even more so in the field of teaching English as a second or additional language. When I ask teachers how they draw attention to language and expanding grammatical complexity, I often get a version of one of these two responses:

1. Ugh, I hate teaching grammar. I don't see the point of it. Exposing students to language and writing through mentor texts naturally supports their understanding and use of increasingly sophisticated writing. If I didn't have to teach it, I wouldn't be able to name the rules or parts of speech, and that doesn't impact my ability to read or write or survive in daily life. Also, it is just boring—I am not making my students diagram sentences and do drill-and-kill verb-tense conjugations.
2. Grammar is so important for supporting reading and writing. When students have vocabulary to talk about and understand the structure of language, they become stronger writers. For multilingual

students, exposure is key, but why wouldn't we also explicitly teach and tell them how the language works? I know people hate the idea of having students conjugate verbs, but would you rather just try to figure it out on your own, or would you rather have someone say, "This is how this works"? It doesn't have to be flash cards and rote work—it can be an explicit introduction to a needed concept followed by authentic application.

What Does the Research Say?

As seen in the vignette, grammar instruction can be polarizing. However, the one thing most educators agree on is that grammar should be explored in opportunities for meaningful listening, speaking, reading, and writing opportunities. The National Council of Teachers of English has a position statement discouraging the use of repetitive grammar drills and exercises because research has documented that teaching grammar in isolation does not improve students' speaking and writing (1985). This research has been documented for decades (McQuade 1980).

Grammar instruction is most beneficial when contextualized within students' reading and writing (Weaver 1996). Instructional recommendations based on grammar research include invitations to notice, label, revise, and imitate grammatical skills (Anderson 2017). For multilingual students, scholars have also documented that effective second language instruction includes a combination of explicit teaching on language features, including syntax and grammar, and extensive opportunities for multilingual students to use this learning in meaningful contexts (Hochman and Wexler 2017; Goldenberg 2008).

Five Instructional Strategies

The following strategies draw on the previously mentioned research by providing a combination of instruction and opportunities for meaningful application. The strategies range from informal approaches to inductive student analysis to more heavily structured sentence expansions, but they *all* include opportunities for applying the learning in context. There is not a sequence for these instructional strategies. They should all be used based on students' needs and be connected with meaningful and authentic oral or writing opportunities to apply the learning about language and grammatical complexity.

STRATEGY 1 Noticing, Naming, and Evaluating with Mentor Texts

Drawing students' attention to language is an easy and important first step to supporting multilingual students. This can also be an opportunity to introduce the academic vocabulary related to grammar and language, such as parts of speech. You can notice and name informally in connection with reading and read-alouds. However, this strategy is related to preplanned instructional scaffolds.

Based on observations of students' oral and written language, identify a common aspect of language or grammatical complexity that would support and enhance students' communication. Use a mentor text to draw attention to the focal concept and encourage students' use of the new concept in speaking or writing. For example, I noticed two needs related to adjectives in a group of second graders' writing. Some of the students were not including any details or description in their writing. Another group of multilingual students were placing the adjective after the noun, a common grammatical approximation for Spanish-speaking students. I wanted to support their descriptive writing and help expand their oral language conversations, so I selected a mentor text that included rich, descriptive language. We had previously read *The Bad Seed*, by Jory John (2017), so they knew the premise of the story and we could focus on noticing the language choices the author made, specifically the use of adjectives.

I opened to the first double-page spread and read aloud, "I'm a bad seed. A baaaaaaaaaaaaaaad seed" (John 2017). I asked students to do a think-pair-share with a partner about the following: "What do you think the author wants us to know about the main character?" The students quickly identified that the author wanted the reader to know the seed was bad. I confirmed and explained that authors often use adjectives—words that describe things, or nouns—to help the reader understand more about what is going on in the story. I told them I was going to read it again, but without the adjective: "I'm a seed. A seed." The children laughed. I told them that I thought this would be a really boring story without the adjectives. I also told them that as a reader and a listener, I wanted to know more about their thinking, and using an adjective before the noun to describe it could be helpful. I told them that authors in all languages use adjectives to provide details. In English, the adjective comes before the noun, but Spanish authors place the adjective after the noun.

I asked students to take out the story they had been working on during writing that week. I told students to reread the story and encouraged them to revise if there was anywhere in the story where they thought adding an adjective before the noun would make their story stronger. Then they shared their work with their partner and discussed how they thought the adjective usage improved their story.

This simple-to-use strategy is quick, situates the grammar and language learning in context, and provides an authentic opportunity for students to try it.

Steps for instruction

1. Identify language or grammar patterns in the class that could benefit from additional support.
2. Select a mentor text that has strong instances of the identified pattern.
3. Model thinking aloud to draw attention to the focal concept, or prompt students with questions to notice and reflect on the focal concept.
4. If needed, provide academic vocabulary to discuss the concept and purpose (parts of speech, tense, sentence structure, etc.).
5. Encourage students to use the pattern in speaking or writing.

STRATEGY 2 Concept Attainment

Concept attainment is an inductive approach to supporting multilingual students in analyzing grammar and writing. Instead of giving students a definition or explicitly teaching them a rule or grammar concept, this strategy involves students in comparing examples and nonexamples. Typically, this takes the form of students working together to place examples in yes and no categories. Then, students generate a definition or characteristics of the concept. For a more scaffolded alternative, the teacher could place the examples in the yes and no categories, and then the students could generate ideas and justification about why each example was in each column.

Like all the strategies, the focal concept should be based on students' needs and what you are observing in speaking and writing. For example, a common grammar challenge I see is subject-verb agreement. A student might say something like, "They is coming to my house on Monday." Based on these grammar approximations, you could provide a concept attainment list like this:

Those people is running fast.
That person is running fast.
The children were tired.
The children was tired.
They is friends.
They are friends.
I am five feet tall.
I are five feet tall.
That boy are nice.
That boy is nice.

Figure 11.1 is a graphic organizer to support the process (see also OR 11–1 in the Online Resources). Students use this as a guide for oral discussion with peers, or they can complete it independently in writing. I love this strategy because you can easily differentiate it, but students do the analysis and teaching about what they notice about how the English language works. This also helps for retention

OR 11-1

CONCEPT ATTAINMENT

Name: ____________________

Categorize the sentences.

Yes	No

Why did you categorize them this way?

What definition, rule, or characteristics can you design to explain this?

What is one more Yes example?

What is one more No example?

FIGURE 11.1 *Concept Attainment* **OR 11-1**

of concepts because they are moving beyond memorization or corrections. Ideally, I ask students to try out the newly defined grammar concept in a conversation with peers or in their writing.

Steps for instruction

1. Identify language or grammar patterns that you have observed students commonly misusing.
2. Create a list of examples and nonexamples related to the pattern or rule.
3. Explain to students that learning a language is difficult, but analyzing patterns can help us better understand the language and support our speaking and writing in a new language.
4. Tell them you generated a list of examples that are a common challenge when learning a language.
5. Give students the concept attainment graphic organizer and ask them to write down their answers while they work with a partner.

6. Tell them to place each sentence in the "Yes" or "No" column.
7. Have students discuss why they categorized them in that way.
8. Ask students to create a definition, rule, or characteristics to explain the yes category.
9. Tell students to create one additional example each for the "Yes" and "No" columns.

STRATEGY 3 Sentence Expansion

The goal of the sentence expansion instructional strategy is to help multilingual students write more detailed sentences with increasingly complex sentence structure. Multilingual students often rely on repetitive sentence structures and can benefit from teachers drawing attention to and providing specific instruction about sentence structures. This can take on varying forms of complexity. Following are three approaches to sentence expansion strategies. One important thing to note is that after the strategy instruction, you should encourage students to apply this learning in an authentic context such as their own conversations or writing.

Strategy 1 A simple way to start is to ask students to help expand a simple sentence and add detail. Then you can model expanding grammatical complexity and punctuation as needed.

For example, I asked students to help me add to and improve my sentence: *The boy ran.* Students shouted out ideas as I revised:

The boy ran to the store.

The boy ran to the store to get candy.

The naughty boy ran to the store to get candy.

After a moment of silence, I prompted: "When did the naughty boy run to the store to get candy?"

A student said, "When he was supposed to be in school!"

I replied, "Oh, that is interesting. Where should we put that? We could put it at the end: *The naughty boy ran to the store to get candy when he was supposed to be in school.* Or, we could put it at the beginning, but we would need some punctuation because *when he was supposed to be in school* is a dependent clause: *When he was supposed to be in school, the naughty boy ran to the store to get candy.*"

Steps for instruction

1. Write a simple sentence or use an example from student writing.
2. Ask students to help you add more detail and expand the sentence.
3. Continue revising the sentence with student suggestions.
4. Prompt with questions when needed to help students add to the sentence.
5. Draw attention to expanding grammatical complexity and model structure options with a brief explanation of the grammar application.

Strategy 2 If students need more structure, explanation, and modeling to create extended or expanded sentences, you can model how to build an extended sentence with a chart that breaks down possibilities, like the one in Figure 11.2.

Number? Type or Kind?	Who or What?	Action?	What?	To or For?	When? Where? How? Why?
Five smart	children	competed	against each other	for the spelling bee championship	in Atlanta, Georgia.
Wild	horses	run	free		in the mountains.

FIGURE 11.2 *Sentence Expansion*

Steps for instruction

1. Create a blank graphic organizer like the one in Figure 11.2.
2. Explain that sentences can be expanded in many ways and model writing a sentence in the graphic organizer.
3. Ask students to work in partners to create an expanded sentence using the graphic organizer.
4. Encourage students to use this when revising their own writing.

Strategy 3 Another version of this activity is a sentence expansion summary. Building on students' learning in a content area, students use newly learned vocabulary in context to create complex and compound sentences. This strategy allows students to reinforce new vocabulary and learning while simultaneously expanding their grammatical complexity usage. I created a scaffolded version of the expansion summary that was connected to a research project on sea life. I highlighted the vocabulary that was introduced prior to reading and created complex and compound sentence stems for the students to use to document their learning.

The clownfish benefits from interacting with anemones, and . . .

The clownfish benefits from interacting with anemones because . . .

The clownfish benefits from interacting with anemones, but . . .

The interaction is beneficial for both the clownfish and the anemones, so . . .

Once students are familiar with using academic vocabulary and creating complex and compound sentences in sentence expansion summaries, they can begin creating their own instead of using the teacher's predetermined structure.

Steps for instruction

1. Identify key content vocabulary.
2. Create a series of sentence expansion summary frames that include vocabulary and target sentence structures.
    a. Depending on students' needs, this can include just compound sentences.
    b. For more of a challenge, it can include complex, compound, and compound-complex sentences.
3. Introduce and preteach content vocabulary.
4. Read together or have students read independently about the content.
5. Ask students to complete the sentence expansion summary.

STRATEGY 4 Analyzing and Upgrading

When you are introducing revision and grammatical concepts, it is helpful for students to see it introduced first in a piece of writing that is not their own. Analyzing and upgrading is an instructional strategy that allows students to draw on and apply their learning of grammar and revision in a text created by the teacher. The teacher-created text should lend itself to multiple, clear opportunities where students could make revisions to upgrade the writing based on writing concepts and grammar that you have introduced. You can model an initial example of the analysis and revision and then ask students to try it individually or in pairs.

Analyzing writing that was written by someone else allows students to be more objective and decreases stress or connection to their writing while they're first learning to apply their revision strategies. For example, we had been working on sentence expansion to include complex and compound sentences in student writing, so I created the following text with multiple opportunities to revise and create complex or compound sentences:

> *It was my birthday. I was very excited to open my presents. The first present was a boring toy. The second present looked like it was moving. I heard a bark. I knew it was the puppy I had been asking for. I raced to the present. I ripped off the wrapping paper. It was a tiny golden retriever. That was exactly what I wanted. I hugged my parents. Then, I thanked my parents. I spent the rest of the day playing with my new puppy.*

We completed the first sentence combination to form a compound sentence together. Then students completed revising the paragraph on their own. Figure 11.3 is a sample student revision.

I have also seen teachers do this exercise with adding adjectives to create noun groups or finding verbs and upgrading them to higher-quality, descriptive verbs. The options are endless but should be based on what you observe as a need in student writing. This strategy also directly connects to the next strategy of having students set goals and apply this work in their own writing and revisions.

Steps for instruction

1. Analyze student writing to identify revision needs specifically related to language and expanding grammatical complexity.
2. If you have not introduced the concept yet, model the concept in the context of writing.
3. Create a text with multiple, clear opportunities for students to make revisions to upgrade the writing based on writing concepts and grammar that you've introduced.
4. Model an initial example of the analysis and revision.
5. Ask students to try it individually or with partners.

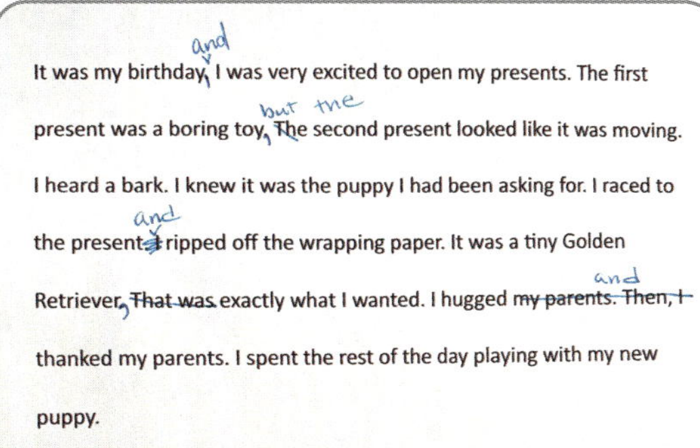
It was my birthday. I was very excited to open my presents. The first present was a boring toy. The second present looked like it was moving. I heard a bark. I knew it was the puppy I had been asking for. I raced to the present. I ripped off the wrapping paper. It was a tiny Golden Retriever. That was exactly what I wanted. I hugged my parents. Then, I thanked my parents. I spent the rest of the day playing with my new puppy.

FIGURE 11.3 *Sentence Combination Example*

STRATEGY 5 Application and Self-Checking

The purpose of modeling, teaching, discussing, and engaging with language and expanding grammatical complexity is to help students understand and use this knowledge in their oral language and writing. Encouraging students to use this knowledge in their writing is an important aspect of supporting students in applying this learning. However, students are often primarily focused on getting their thinking down on paper during their first draft of writing. Because of this, providing focused and scaffolded opportunities to apply this learning during self-editing and revision can be empowering and helpful for enhancing the complexity of multilingual students' writing.

When asking multilingual students to apply grammatical concepts when reading and revising their own writing, providing a checklist or guide with supports such as examples, visuals, and color-coding can be helpful. This is a simple strategy to offer reinforcement of previously introduced concepts. The concrete nature of the checklist or guide will help students identify opportunities to revise and enhance their writing based on what they have learned. I recommend having students put a star or check mark next to each item in the self-check once they have identified where they have it in the text or where they revised to accomplish the item on the checklist.

Figure 11.4 is an example of a self-check for analyzing students' written endings of a narrative. This check includes essential content for writing a quality ending: Is it rushed? Does it wrap up thoughtfully? Are the where and when clear? The second part of this self-check includes a focus on the grammatical instructional points that were addressed in class to support student writing.

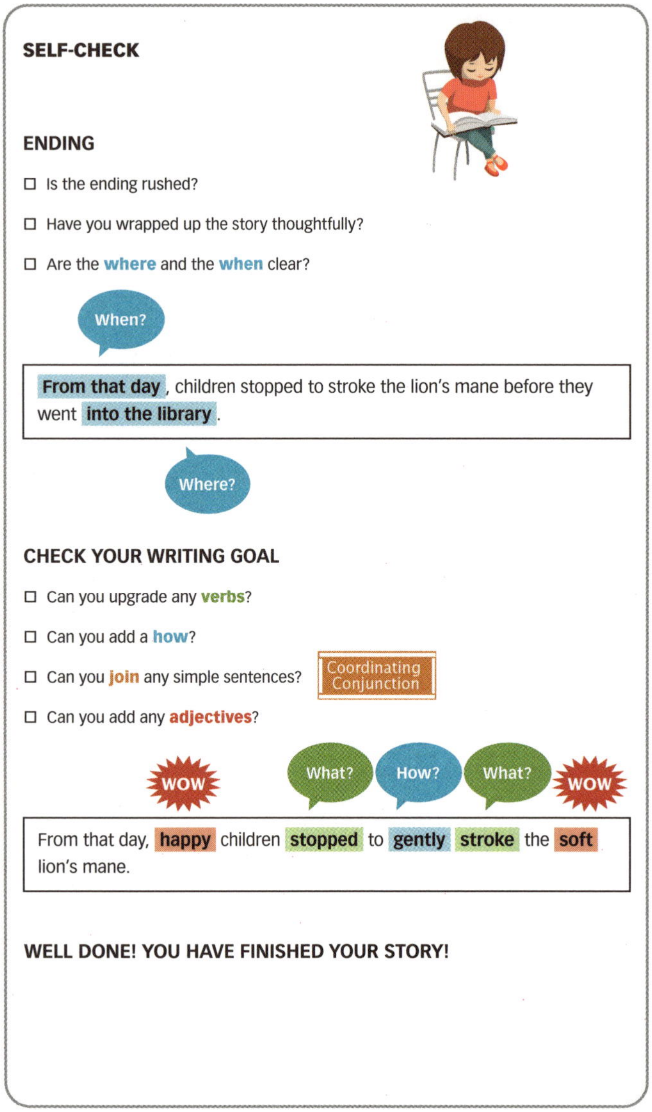

SELF-CHECK

ENDING

- ☐ Is the ending rushed?
- ☐ Have you wrapped up the story thoughtfully?
- ☐ Are the **where** and the **when** clear?

When?

From that day, children stopped to stroke the lion's mane before they went **into the library**.

Where?

CHECK YOUR WRITING GOAL

- ☐ Can you upgrade any **verbs**?
- ☐ Can you add a **how**?
- ☐ Can you **join** any simple sentences? Coordinating Conjunction
- ☐ Can you add any **adjectives**?

WOW What? How? What? WOW

From that day, **happy** children **stopped** to **gently** **stroke** the **soft** lion's mane.

WELL DONE! YOU HAVE FINISHED YOUR STORY!

FIGURE 11.4 *Self-Check*

Steps for instruction

1. Identify key writing and grammatical concepts that you have introduced during the current writing unit or instructional focus.
2. Create a student-friendly and language-appropriate guide or self-check for students. When possible, include additional scaffolds such as symbols, visuals, colors, and examples.

3. Introduce and model using the self-check to make revisions and enhance the writing complexity.
4. Ask students to use the checklist to assist with revisions.
5. Optional: Encourage students to review and discuss their checklists and writing with a partner.

Strategies in Action: Primary-Grade Differentiated Grammar Goals

While conducting research in Australia, I was impressed with the way educators introduced and talked about functional grammar. I never observed teachers lecturing, quizzing, or doing decontextualized lessons related to grammar. Instead, educators used the language of grammar to help support students' writing and ability to clearly communicate their stories. Tam Jarowyj, a second-grade teacher in Australia, seamlessly weaved attention to language and expanding grammatical complexity throughout her reading and writing instruction. In addition, she provided ongoing differentiation and goal setting depending on students' linguistic needs and levels of proficiency.

Each student had individualized goals related to writing and the functional grammar instruction. For example, all students had a goal of upgrading verbs and adding adjectives for description. Students who were ready for the challenge of using compound sentences would add that to their writing goals. Tam continually encouraged students to return to their goals when writing or revising. Tam taught a modified and more complex version of the analyze and upgrade strategy with her students. As you can see in Figures 11.5 and 11.6, Tam created instructions for analyzing and upgrading with multiple goals: descriptive detail, strong verbs, compound sentences, and noun groups. However, she also noted in the instructions, "Let your writing goal guide you." This allowed for differentiation so all students could work at their appropriate linguistic levels.

One student added descriptive detail, created noun groups, and reduced repetitive wording, but was not yet ready to combine sentences (see Figure 11.5). Figure 11.6 shows an example from a student whose goals included upgrading verbs, adding descriptive details, creating noun groups, and creating compound sentences. I love how all students worked in their area of challenge and had differentiated focuses in terms of language and grammatical complexity.

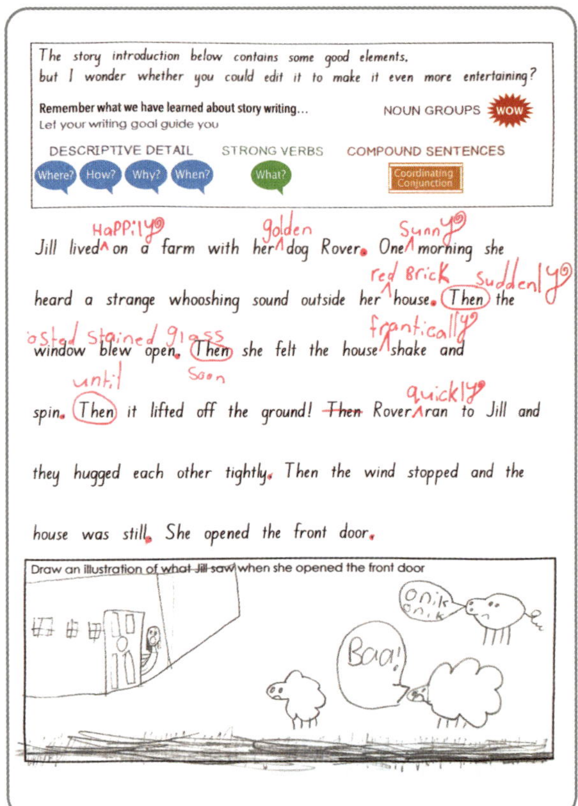

FIGURE 11.5 *Student Example 1*

FIGURE 11.6 *Student Example 2*

REFLECTION QUESTIONS

3. What types of opportunities to draw attention to language and expanding grammatical complexity are you currently including in your instruction?
4. What are some successes you have had with drawing attention to language and expanding grammatical complexity?
5. What are some challenges you have had with drawing attention to language and expanding grammatical complexity?
6. What strategies from this chapter could you add to your literacy instruction to better support your multilingual students?
7. How could you adapt one or more of these strategies to fit the needs of your multilingual students?

WORKS CITED

Allington, Richard. 1991. "Children Who Find Learning to Read Difficult: School Responses to Diversity." In *Literacy for a Diverse Society: Perspectives, Practices, and Policies*, edited by Elfrieda H. Hiebert, 237–52. New York: Teachers College Press.

Anderson, Jeff. 2017. *Patterns of Power: Inviting Young Writers into the Conventions of Language, Grades 1–5*. With Whitney La Rocca. Portland, ME: Stenhouse.

August, Diane, Lee Branum-Martin, Elsa Cardenas-Hagan, and David J. Francis. 2009. "The Impact of an Instructional Intervention on the Science and Language Learning of Middle Grade English Language Learners." *Journal of Research on Educational Effectiveness* 2 (4): 345–76.

August, Diane, Diane Staehr Fenner, and Sydney Snyder. 2014. "Scaffolding Instruction for English Language Learners: A Resource Guide for English Language Arts." Washington, DC: American Institutes for Research.

August, Diane, and Timothy Shanahan. 2006. *Developing Literacy in Second-Language Learners: Report of the National Literacy Panel on Language-Minority Children and Youth*. New York: Routledge.

Baker, Scott, Nonie Lesaux, Madhavi Jayanthi, Joseph Dimino, C. Patrick Proctor, Joan Morris, Russell Gersten, Kelly Haymond, Michael Kieffer, Sylvia Linan-Thompson, and Rebecca Newman-Gonchar. 2014. *Teaching Academic Content and Literacy to English Learners in Elementary and Middle School* (NCEE 2014-4012). Washington, DC: National Center of Education Evaluation and Regional Assistance (NCEE), Institute for Education Sciences, US Department of Education.

Barton, Angela Calabrese, and Edna Tan. 2009. "Funds of Knowledge and Discourses and Hybrid Space." *Journal of Research in Science Teaching* 46 (1): 50–73.

Beck, Isabel L., Margaret G. McKeown, and Linda Kucan. 2013. *Bringing Words to Life: Robust Vocabulary Instruction*. New York: Guilford.

Beers, Kylene. 2002. *When Kids Can't Read—What Teachers Can Do: A Guide for Teachers 6–12*. Portsmouth, NH: Heinemann.

Bernhardt, Elizabeth. 2011. *Understanding Advanced Second-Language Reading*. New York: Routledge.

Bialik, Kristen, Alissa Scheller, and Kristi Walker. 2018. "6 Facts About English Language Learners in U.S. Public Schools." Pew Research Center. https://www.pewresearch.org/short-reads/2018/10/25/6-facts-about-english-language-learners-in-u-s-public-schools/#:~:text=While%20these%20are%20among%20the,%25)%20and%20Wisconsin%20(15%25).

Bialystok, Ellen. 2011. "Reshaping the Mind: The Benefits of Bilingualism." *Canadian Journal of Experimental Psychology / Revue canadienne de psychologie expérimentale* 65 (4): 229–35. https://doi.org/10.1037/a0025406.

Calderón, Margarita, Diane August, Daniel Durán, Nancy Madden, Robert Slavin, and Maria Gil. 2003. *Spanish to English Transitional Reading: Teacher's Manual*. Baltimore, MD: Success for All Foundation.

Calhoun, Emily. 1999. *Teaching Beginning Reading and Writing with the Picture Word Inductive Model*. Alexandria, VA: ASCD.

Carlisle, Joanne F. 2003. "Morphology Matters in Learning to Read: A Commentary." *Reading Psychology* 24 (3–4): 291–322. https://doi.org/10.1080/02702710390227369.

Chang, Wan-Chen, and Yu-Min Ku. 2015. "The Effects of Note-Taking Skills Instruction on Elementary Students' Reading." *Journal of Educational Research* 108 (4): 278–91.

Cook, Vivian. 2001. "Using the First Language in the Classroom." *Canadian Modern Language Review* 57 (3): 402–23.

Correia, Amy. 2020. "Flip the Script: English Learners Aren't Underperforming—We Are Underserving: A Move from Deficit Thinking to Democratic Education." In *Social Justice and Putting Theory into*

Practice in Schools and Communities, edited by Susan Trostle Brand and Lori E. Ciccomascolo, 81–93. Hershey, PA: IGI Global.

Cummins, James. 2000. *Language, Power, and Pedagogy: Bilingual Children in the Crossfire.* Clevedon, UK: Multilingual Matters.

———. 2005. "A Proposal for Action: Strategies for Recognizing Heritage Language Competence as a Learning Resource Within the Mainstream Classroom." *Modern Language Journal* 89 (4): 585–92.

Cunningham, Thomas H., and C. Ray Graham. 2000. "Increasing Native English Vocabulary Recognition Through Spanish Immersion: Cognate Transfer from Foreign to First Language." *Journal of Educational Psychology* 92 (1): 37–49.

Darling-Hammond, Linda. 1995. "Inequality and Access to Knowledge." In *Handbook of Research on Multicultural Education*, edited by James A. Banks, 465–83. New York: Macmillan.

Davidson, Sean J., and Rollanda E. O'Connor. 2019. "An Intervention Using Morphology to Derive Word Meanings for English Language Learners." *Journal of Applied Behavior Analysis* 52 (2): 394–407.

Duffelmeyer, Frederick A. 1994. "Effective Anticipation Guide Statements for Learning from Expository Prose." *Journal of Reading* 37 (6): 452–57.

Duke, Nell, and P. David Pearson. 2009. "Effective Practices for Developing Reading Comprehension." *Journal of Education* 189 (1–2): 107–22.

Echevarria, Jana, Deborah Short, and Kristin Powers. 2006. "School Reform and Standards-Based Education: A Model for English-Language Learners." *Journal of Educational Research* 99 (4): 195–210.

Echevarria, Jana, and MaryEllen Vogt. 2010. *Response to Intervention (RTI) and English Learners: Making It Happen.* Boston: Allyn and Bacon.

Echevarria, Jana, MaryEllen Vogt, and Deborah J. Short. 2007. *Making Content Comprehensible for English Learners: The SIOP Model.* 3rd ed. Boston: Allyn and Bacon.

Escamilla, Kathy, Susan Hopewell, Sandra Butvilofsky, Wendy Sparrow, Lucinda Soltero-González, Olivia Ruiz-Figueroa, and Manuel Escamilla. 2014. *Biliteracy from the Start: Literacy Squared in Action.* Philadelphia: Caslon.

Fenner, Diane Staehr. 2019. "Scaffolding Instruction for English Learners (Part 1)." *Education.com* (blog), January 28, https://blog.education.com/2019/01/28/elscaffoldingpart1/.

Fisher, Douglas, and Nancy Frey. 2008. *Word Wise and Content Rich: Five Essential Steps to Teaching Academic Vocabulary.* Portsmouth, NH: Heinemann.

Flowerdew, John. 1994. "Research of Relevance to Second Language Lecture Comprehension: An Overview." In *Academic Listening: Research Perspectives*, edited by John Flowerdew, 7–29. Cambridge UK: Cambridge University Press.

Frayer, Dorothy A., Wayne C. Frederick, and Herbert J. Klausmeier. 1969. *A Schema for Testing the Level of Concept Mastery.* Technical report no. 16. Madison, WI: University of Wisconsin Research and Development Center for Cognitive Learning.

Gambrell, Linda. 1983. "The Occurrence of Think-Time During Reading Comprehension Instruction." *Journal of Educational Research* 77 (2): 77–80.

García, Ofelia. 2020. "Translanguaging and Latinx Bilingual Readers." *Reading Teacher* 73 (5): 557–62.

Gentile, Lance. 2004. *The Oracy Instructional Guide.* Carlsbad, CA: Dominie Press.

Gibbons, Pauline. 2002. *Scaffolding Language, Scaffolding Learning: Teaching Second Language Learners in the Mainstream Classroom.* Portsmouth, NH: Heinemann.

———. 2009. *English Learners, Academic Literacy, and Thinking: Learning in the Challenge Zone.* Portsmouth, NH: Heinemann.

Goldenberg, Claude. 2008. "Teaching English Language Learners: What the Research Does— and Does Not—Say." *American Educator* (Summer): 8–23, 42–44. https://www.aft.org/sites/default/files/goldenberg.pdf.

———. 2013. "Unlocking the Research on English Learners: What We Know—and Don't Yet Know—About Effective Instruction." *America Educator* 37 (2): 4–11, 38.

Gonzalez, Norma, Luis C. Moll, and Cathy Amanti, eds. 2005. *Funds of Knowledge*. New York: Routledge.

Goodman, Bridget, and Serikbolsyn Tastanbek. 2021. "Making the Shift from a Codeswitching to a Translanguaging Lens in English Language Teacher Education." *TESOL Quarterly* 55 (1): 29–53.

Griffiths, Roger. 1990. "Speech Rate and NNS Comprehension: A Preliminary Study in Time-Benefit Analysis." *Language Learning* 40 (3): 311–36.

Grosjean, François. 2010. *Bilingual: Life and Reality*. Cambridge, MA: Harvard University Press.

Hakuta, Kenji, and Maria Santos. 2012. "Understanding Language: Challenges and Opportunities for Language Learning in the Context of Common Core State Standards and Next Generation Science Standards." Paper presented at the Understanding Language: Language, Literacy, and Learning in the Content Areas Conference, Stanford University, April. https://ul.stanford.edu/sites/default/files/resource/2021-03/Conference%20Summary_FINAL_Nov2012.pdf.

Harvey, Stephanie, and Anne Goudvis. 2000. *Strategies That Work: Teaching Comprehension for Understanding and Engagement*. Portland, ME: Stenhouse.

Haydon, Todd, G. Richmond Mancil, Stephen D. Kroeger, James McLeskey, and Wan-Yu Jenny Lin. 2011. "A Review of the Effectiveness of Guided Notes for Students Who Struggle Learning Academic Content." *Preventing School Failure: Alternative Education for Children and Youth* 55 (4): 226–31.

Herber, Harold. 1978. *Teaching Reading in Content Areas*. Englewood Cliffs, NJ: Prentice-Hall.

Hindman, Annemarie, Barbara Wasik, and Donald Bradley. 2018. "The Question Is Just the Beginning: How Head Start Teachers Use Wait Time and Feedback During Book Reading." Paper presented at the annual meeting of the American Educational Research Association, New York, April.

Hochman, Judith C., and Natalie Wexler. 2017. "One Sentence at a Time: The Need for Explicit Instruction in Teaching Students to Write Well." *American Educator* 41 (2): 30–37, 43.

Ilomo, Onesto, and Sabela Mjini Ilomo. 2021. "The Use of Visual Aids in Supporting English Language Teaching in English Medium Primary Schools: A Case Study in Meru District." *International Journal of Contemporary Applied Researches* 8 (5): 27–41.

Jiménez, Robert T., Sam David, Keenan Fagan, Victoria J. Risko, Mark Pacheco, Lisa Pray, and Mark Gonzales. 2015. "Using Translation to Drive Conceptual Development for Students Becoming Literate in English as an Additional Language." *Research in the Teaching of English* 49: 248–71.

John, Jory. 2017. *The Bad Seed.* Illustrated by Pete Oswald. New York: HarperCollins Children's Books.

Johnson, David W., Roger T. Johnson, and Karl A. Smith. 1991. *Active Learning: Cooperation in the College Classroom.* Edina, MN: Interaction Book Company.

Kagan, Spencer, and Miguel Kagan. 2009. *Kagan Cooperative Learning.* San Clemente, CA: Kagan Cooperative Learning.

Kang, Shumin. 2004. "Using Visual Organizers to Enhance EFL Instruction." *ELT Journal* 58 (1): 58–67.

Kieffer, Michael J., and Nonie Lesaux. 2008. "The Role of Derivational Morphology in the Reading Comprehension of Spanish-Speaking English Language Learners." *Reading and Writing* 21 (8): 783–804.

Kiewra, Kenneth A. 2002. "How Classroom Teachers Can Help Students Learn and Teach Them How to Learn." *Theory into Practice* 41 (2): 71–80.

Krashen, Stephen. 2003. *Explorations in Language Acquisition and Use: The Taipei Lectures.* Portsmouth, NH: Heinemann.

Lave, Jean, and Etienne Wenger. 1991. *Situated Learning: Legitimate Peripheral Participation.* Cambridge, UK: Cambridge University Press.

Lesaux, Nonie, Michael J. Kieffer, Elisabeth S. Faller, and Joan G. Kelley. 2010. "The Effectiveness and Ease of Implementation of an Academic Vocabulary Intervention for Linguistically Diverse Students in Urban Middle Schools." *Reading Research Quarterly* 45 (2): 196–228.

Lyman, Frank. 1981. "The Responsive Classroom Discussion: The Inclusion of All Students." In *Mainstreaming Digest*, edited by Audrey Springs Anderson, 109–13. College Park, MD: University of Maryland Press.

Marsh, Valerie L. 2018. *Best Practices for Educating English Language Learners: History, Controversy, and a Path Forward*. Research brief. Rochester, NY: Center for Urban Education Success, the Warner School of Education, University of Rochester. https://www.rochester.edu/warner/cues/wp-content/uploads/2018/10/ELLS-brief_FINAL-.pdf.

Marzano, Robert J., and Debra J. Pickering. 2005. *Building Academic Vocabulary: Teacher's Manual*. Alexandria, VA: ASCD.

Marzano, Robert J., Debra Pickering, and Jane E. Pollock. 2001. *Classroom Instruction That Works: Research-Based Strategies for Increasing Student Achievement*. Alexandria, VA: ASCD.

Matsuura, Hiroko, Reiko Chiba, Sean Mahoney, and Sarah Rilling. 2014. "Accent and Speech Rate Effects in English as a Lingua Franca." *System* 46: 143–50.

Maybin, Janet, Neil Mercer, and Barry Stierer. 1992. "'Scaffolding' Learning in the Classroom." In *Thinking Voices: The Work of the National Oracy Project*, edited by Kate Norman, 186–95. London: Hodder and Stoughton.

McGregor, Tanny. 2018. *Ink and Ideas: Sketchnotes for Engagement, Comprehension, and Thinking*. Portsmouth, NH: Heinemann.

McQuade, Finlay. 1980. "Examining a Grammar Course: The Rationale and the Result." *English Journal* 69 (7): 26–30.

Moll, Luis C., Cathy Amanti, Deborah Neff, and Norma Gonzalez. 1992. "Funds of Knowledge for Teaching: Using a Qualitative Approach to Connect Homes and Classrooms." *Theory into Practice* 31 (2): 132–41.

Moses, Lindsey, and Carolina Torrejon Capurro. 2023. "Literacy-Based Play with Young Emergent Bilinguals: Explorations in Vocabulary, Translanguaging, and Identity Work." *TESOL Quarterly*, May 31. https://doi.org/10.1002/tesq.3236.

Moses, Lindsey, Matt Hajdun, and Ana Alvarado Aguirre. 2021. "Translanguaging Together: Building Bilingual Identities con Nuevos Amigos." *Reading Teacher* 75 (3): 291–304.

Moses, Lindsey, and Laura Beth Kelly. 2017. "The Development of Positive Literate Identities Among Emerging Bilingual and Monolingual First Graders." *Journal of Literacy Research* 49 (3): 393–423. https://doi.org/10.1177/1086296X17713291.

———. 2018. "'We're a Little Loud. That's Because We Like to Read!': Developing Positive Views of Reading in a Diverse, Urban First Grade." *Journal of Early Childhood Literacy* 18 (3): 307–37. https://doi.org/10.1177/1468798416662513.

National Center for Education Statistics. 2023. "English Learners in Public Schools." *Condition of Education*. Washington, DC: Institute for Education Sciences, US Department of Education. https://nces.ed.gov/programs/coe/indicator/cgf/english-learners.

National Council of Teachers of English. 1985. "Resolution on Grammar Exercises to Teach Speaking and Writing." NCTE. November 30. https://ncte.org/statement/grammarexercises/.

National Reading Panel. 2000. *Teaching Children to Read: An Evidence-Based Assessment of the Scientific Research Literature on Reading and Its Implications for Reading Instruction*. Washington, DC: National Institute of Child Health and Human Development.

Ogle, Donna M. 1986. "K-W-L: A Teaching Model That Develops Active Reading of Expository Text." *Reading Teacher* 39 (6): 564–70.

Paris, Django. 2012. "Culturally Sustaining Pedagogy: A Needed Change in Stance, Terminology, and Practice." *Educational Researcher* 41 (3): 93–97.

Rahmani, Mina, and Karim Sadeghi. 2011. "Effects of Note-Taking Training on Reading Comprehension and Recall." *Reading Matrix* 11 (2): 116–28.

Ruiz-de-Velasco, Jorge, and Michael Fix. 2000. "Overlooked and Underserved: Immigrant Students in U.S. Secondary Schools." Washington, DC: The Urban Institute.

Saunders, William M., and Claude Goldenberg. 2007. "The Effects of an Instructional Conversation on English Language Learners' Concepts of Friendship and Story Comprehension." In *Talking Texts: How Speech and Writing Interact in School Learning*, edited by Rosalind Horowitz, 221–52. Mahwah, NJ: Erlbaum.

Sayer, Peter. 2013. "Translanguaging, TexMex, and Bilingual Pedagogy: Emergent Bilinguals Learning Through the Vernacular." *TESOL Quarterly* 47 (1): 63–88.

Serravallo, Jennifer. 2015. *The Reading Strategies Book: Your Everything Guide to Developing Skilled Readers.* Portsmouth, NH: Heinemann.

Shanahan, Timothy, Kim Callison, Christine Carriere, Nell Duke, P. David Pearson, Christopher Schatschneider, and Joseph Torgesen. 2010. *Improving Reading Comprehension in Kindergarten Through 3rd Grade: IES Practice Guide* (NCEE 2010-4038). Washington, DC: National Center of Education Evaluation and Regional Assistance, Institute for Education Sciences, US Department of Education.

Stead, Tony. 2005. *Reality Checks: Teaching Reading Comprehension with Nonfiction.* Portland, ME: Stenhouse.

Subero, David, Ellen Vujasinović, and Moises Esteban-Guitart. 2017. "Mobilizing Funds of Identity in and out of School." *Cambridge Journal of Education* 47 (2): 247–63.

Taba, Hilda. 1967. *Teacher's Handbook for Elementary Social Studies.* Reading, MA: Addison-Wesley.

Thomas, Michael, and Hayo Reinders. 2010. "Deconstructing Tasks and Technology." In *Task-Based Language Learning and Teaching with Technology*, edited by Michael Thomas and Hayo Reinders, 1–16. London: Continuum.

Udaya, Muthyala. 2021. "Using Semantic Maps as a Teaching Strategy for Vocabulary Development." *European Journal of English Language Teaching* 6 (5): 193–205.

Vygotsky, Lev. 1978/1995. *Mind in Society.* Cambridge, MA: Harvard University Press.

Weaver, Constance. 1996. "Teaching Grammar in the Context of Writing." *English Journal* 85 (7): 15–24.

Wei, Li. 2018. "Translanguaging as a Practical Theory of Language." *Applied Linguistics* 39 (1): 9–30.

Wertsch, James. 1998. *Mind as Action.* New York: Oxford University Press.

WIDA Consortium. 2007. *English Language Proficiency Standards PreKindergarten Through Grade 5*. Madison, WI: Board of Regents of the University of Wisconsin System. https://wida.wisc.edu/sites/default/files/resource/2007-ELPS-PreK-5.pdf.

———. 2012. *2012 Amplification of the English Language Development Standards: Kindergarten–Grade 12*. Madison, WI: Board of Regents of the University of Wisconsin System. https://wida.wisc.edu/sites/default/files/resource/2012-ELD-Standards.pdf.

Wisconsin Department of Public Instruction. n.d. "Semantic Maps for Morphological Analysis." https://dpi.wi.gov/sites/default/files/imce/ela/bank/6-12_L.VAU_Semantic_Maps_for_Morphological_Analysis.pdf.

Wood, David, Jerome Bruner, and Gail Ross. 1976. "The Role of Tutoring in Problem Solving." *Journal of Child Psychology and Psychiatry* 17 (2): 89–100.

Yaqubi, Bager, and Mostafa Pourhaji Rokni. 2012. "Teachers' Limited Wait-Time Practice and Learners' Participation Opportunities in EFL Classroom Interaction." *Journal of English Language Teaching and Learning* 4 (10): 127–61.

Yule, George. 2010. *The Study of Language.* 4th ed. Cambridge, UK: Cambridge University Press.

Acknowledgments continued from the copyright page:

Performance definitions for the levels of English Language Proficiency—chart from p. iii, excerpted from *The WIDA English Language Proficiency Standards,* 2007 Edition, PreKindergarten through Grade 12, used under license from the Board of Regents of the University of Wisconsin System on behalf of the UW–Madison Wisconsin Center for Education Research. All rights reserved.

RAN Chart reproduced from *Reality Checks: Teaching Reading Comprehension with Nonfiction,* 1st Edition by Tony Stead, published by Routledge. Copyright © 2005, reproduced by arrangement with Taylor & Francis Group.

"Semantic Maps for Morphological Analysis," Wisconsin Department of Public Instruction. Used with permission.

Photo from p. 67 and image from p. 144 of *What Are the Rest of My Kids Doing? Fostering Independence in the K–2 Reading Workshop* by Lindsey Moses and Meredith Ogden. Copyright © 2017 by Lindsey Moses and Meredith Ogden. Published by Heinemann, Portsmouth, NH. Reprinted by permission of the Publisher. All rights reserved.

Image Credits

Figure 2.5: ©subjug/iStock/Getty Images/HIP (sticky notes)
Figure 4.7: ©big_and_serious/Adobe Stock (students); ©Andrew Roberts Illustration/Houghton Mifflin Harcourt/HIP (pencil)
Figure 5.3: ©alekseyvanin/Adobe Stock (arms)
Figure 5.6: ©robuart/Shutterstock/HIP
Pages 88, 89: ©Houghton Mifflin Harcourt/HIP (flowers)
Pages 90, 91: ©Art Alex/Adobe Stock (steaming pot)
Figure 7.6 and OR 7–2: ©Houghton Mifflin Harcourt/HIP (child)
Figures 7.9–7.11: ©mutsuMaks/Shutterstock
Figure 7.14: HIP (menu items)
Figure 8.4: ©Anatolii/Adobe Stock (zoo, café, and museum); ©WinWin/Adobe Stock (mall and cinema); ©GreenSkyStudio/Adobe Stock (park)
Figure 8.11: ©Houghton Mifflin Harcourt/HIP (pebble, rock, boulder)
Figures 9.1, 9.2, 9.4, 9.5: ©Tenstudio/Adobe Stock (girl thinking)
Figure 9.1: ©yarrowbuttercup/Adobe Stock (pair of students); ©lisitsa_/Fotolia/HIP (group of students)
Figure 9.2: ©BNP Design Studio/Adobe Stock (boy whispering); ©Kirastock/Shutterstock (girl whispering); ©vector graphics/Adobe Stock (raised hands)
Figures 9.4 and 9.5: ©solthanya/Adobe Stock (two hands); ©zaurrahimov/Adobe Stock (repeat symbol)
Figures 10.1 and 10.2: ©MicroOne/Adobe Stock (biology symbol); ©ONYXprj/Adobe Stock (notepad); ©NWM/Adobe Stock (hand); ©Houghton Mifflin Harcourt/HIP (scribble)
Figure 11.4: ©robu_s/Adobe Stock (student)